River Flowing Home

River
Flowing
Home

A Creative Journey

SUSAN HALL

*For Pat and Eddie,
much love,
Susan Hall*

Green Bridge Press
Point Reyes Station, California

ISBN 978-0-9721120-4-8

Green Bridge Press
P.O. Box 37
Point Reyes Station, California 94956
www.SusanHallArt.com

All artwork and photographs by Susan Hall
unless otherwise specified.

Frontispiece: River Flowing Home, 2008. Oil on linen.
11" × 16". Collection of Laurie Monserrat.

William Stafford, "Any Journey" from *The Way It is: New and Selected Poems.*
Copyright © 1973, 1998 by William Stafford and the Estate of William Stafford.
Reprinted with the permission of Graywolf Press, Minneapolis, Minnesota.
www.graywolfpress.org

Printed in China
First printing 2010

To Marie and Carl Dern

Any Journey

When God watches you walk, you are
neither straight nor crooked. The journey
stretches out, and all of its reasons
beat like a heart. Coming back, no triumph,
no regret, you fold into the curves,
left, right, and arrive. You touch
the door. The road straightens behind you.
It is now. It has all come true.

— *William Stafford*

River Flowing Home

Chapter one

My earliest memories are of wading in a stream behind my house. I remember looking into this stream and being shocked by the icy water; its clarity, the mystifying shapes of the pebbles and five-fingered ferns that embraced its boundaries, and its sound. I had no doubt that this was paradise. This was the birth of my imagination through the senses. I felt wonder, delight, awe. I marveled at the infinite range of each sense; the sound and the absence of sound, the wonder of silence, the enormity of a single rustling leaf entering that silence. So it was with each sense and most of all with sight. Sight seemed to be the integrating compass needle that magnetized and created order out of sensual disarray.

This was the birthplace of my inner vision, which was stimulated and sparked by the vastness of the outer world. This was the beginning of my ability to hold images and thoughts in my mind. Since I was alone a lot and played endlessly out of doors, my fertile imagination was delighted by the companionship I found in the natural world around me.

I appreciated the spirit of this world. I was happy.

I was born in 1943 and raised in the small town of Point Reyes Station at the western edge of Marin County, California. My parents moved to the area in the early Depression years of the 1930s. My father worked much of the rest of his life at a ship-to-shore radio station at the far end of the Point Reyes Peninsula near the lighthouse. In those days, West Marin was inhabited mostly by ranchers and fishermen. The Point Reyes Peninsula, an isolated and wild area, had a profound effect on my identity and development.

During the first few years of my life, my parents, my older sister JoAnn, and I lived in an old white farm house on the edge of Paper Mill Creek, which meanders through the wetlands adjoining Tomales Bay. The white house was torn down long ago, but the wide creek in front is still named White House Pool.

Facing: The Beginning: Papermill Creek and White House Pool.
Top: Old Ranch House, White House Pool.

Daisy and me, 1949.

In 1946, when I was three years old, we moved from the old farm house to three acres in Point Reyes Station a mile away, where my parents built a home. This was a new world of pasture and grass. It was so different from the deep woods and shadows and streams. I loved burrowing in the grass, making forts and huts in the new mown hay. Whatever my mood, I could find a sanctuary in this vast space that would energize and inspire me. If I wanted to, I could lie in the grassy pasture and watch the sky for hours or dig a hole to China looking for treasures. I always found treasures—a scrap of paper, an odd stone, or insects.

My home was like a medieval garden protected by a wall that ensured that life inside was unharmed. This yard I grew up in and returned to many years later taught me that the universe was unlimited even in the smallest spaces.

I discovered and admired worlds within worlds.

Very early, I discovered I loved the process of putting crayon or paint to paper. This became the bridge between my outer and inner worlds. I loved the images in my mind and putting to paper what I saw in my imagination. I remember drawing our cow, Daisy, and feeling bored. It was too easy to copy from reality. It seemed to flatten out the intensity of my inner feelings.

Since I had no art instruction, there was no "right way." I was entering a great mystery, and it felt good to be exploring something unknown. Each line or color or shape seemed to be carved out of the vastness of my interior and exterior life. I trusted that the marks I put on the page, the ones that felt good could be continued. Every evening I sat at the dining room table and drew. Over the years, I wore off the finish of the table through my habitual efforts. I drew whatever I felt like drawing. Although my first-grade teacher was supportive, I don't rememember my other teachers paying that much attention to my artistic endeavors. After all, dealing with four grades at a time in a two-room school house didn't allow for much individual attention. Complete chaos

Point Reyes Station from White House Pool, 1950.

Top: Hotel Point Reyes, 1917.

Left: The White House at White House pool.

Above: White House Pool, early 1900s.

Clockwise from top left: My mother, Avis, and Daisy; JoAnn and me;
my father with the catch of the day; mountain lion, Point Reyes Station, 1935.

was the norm among the forty students, and since I was the only one in my grade, I was often ignored. But being left alone gave me the opportunity to draw.

Drawing was more meaningful to me than speaking because it felt deeper somehow. Drawing carried emotional content that I couldn't articulate. It was a comforting ritual. My father and I seldom spoke, even though he bought me paper, paints, and other art supplies. My mother was vague, preoccupied. She seemed to be happy with me, perhaps because I found so many ways of occupying myself and not bothering her. I do have sweet, fond memories of helping her hang clothes on the line, working in the yard, shelling peas in a big bowl in the sunshine, and cutting flowers with her in the yard. Meanwhile, my sister Jo Ann, four years older, was absorbed with school and her playmates.

I believe my spiritual development began with the incredible awe I felt around me for the natural world. In a mostly Roman Catholic community, my parents supported the ill-attended Presbyterian Church next door to our property. Often our family was the only one present to hear yet another student minister stumble through a sermon. When other members of the congregation showed up, I observed them with fascination. I remember watching an old man take out his false teeth and hold them in his hand. This event was as important to me as communion. Although I was not particularly religious, my father's gift to me of a King James Bible also gave expression to my feelings of fascination and awe. In it, Jesus' words were written in red, as if written in blood. I loved the Psalms, particularly ones of praise. I recall feeling expanded and heartful when I read them.

Blessed are the pure in heart, for they shall see God.

For me, art was special and calming. It was a release from stress and anxiety. It was a companion and friend. The questions I had about life could find expression in my work. Maybe they went unanswered but did not go unexpressed.

These first ten years established a relationship with art that has sustained me all of my life. Art as companion, art as self-expression, art as a means for exploring the great mystery and the unknown, art as a form of gratitude for the beauty around me, has provided me with solace, vitality, replenishment, and passion.

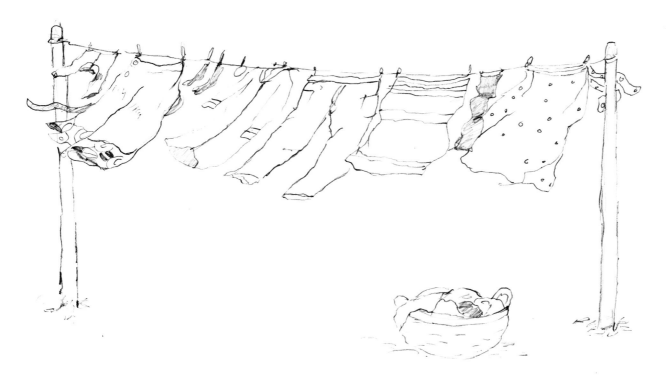

Chapter Two

Today there's a sign on the outskirts of Point Reyes Station that hasn't been changed since the 1950s; it reads, "Population 350." Out of the 350 there were only four or five children my age. Two of them were identical twins and my best friends. I loved being with them since it meant my companionship was doubled. One was quiet, the other more social. When I was with them, I felt I was seeing the two sides of myself. We were out of doors from early morning to evening: walking through sheep pastures and climbing high into giant cypress trees to share secrets with the wind. There were groves of eucalyptus trees planted by early settlers in long straight rows on the edge of town that we loved walking through. After storms, thin bark banners stripped by the wind fluttered in the tree corridors and crunched satisfyingly under foot.

Sometimes we would sit on the steps of the feed store and count the cars as they drove past. On some afternoons, we counted no more than five or six. In the late hot summer we swam in Paper Mill Creek. The big black and white Holstein cows ambled to the water's edge for a drink or slumbered under the willows in the the summer heat. An occasional snort or sneeze would startle me from swimming. I would raise my head out of the water like a seal, alert to the sound that disturbed the quiet.

If I kept my eyes right at water level and looked out beyond the bay where the creek entered, I could imagine where the heavens began. Looking out to the horizon I could see the indistinct fusion of the mouth of the bay with the sky. This all-inclusive experience filled me from head to toe with goose bumps. I could feel my heart ache and was only relieved of the intensity when a fish nibble brought me back to the present moment.

This is one of the poems I wrote when I was twelve about the magic of the creek:

Facing: Horses, Point Reyes Station, 1960.

Creek meandering through

Meadow and sky of blue

Blissfully teasing the fish

That are seizing

The flies that lie low

Where the swift water flows.

Rizzo, 1955.

Odd and quirky individuals were common in Point Reyes and, for the most part, accepted. Old Man Rizzo painted his yard and everything in it with bright silver-aluminum colored paint. His silvery yard was a forlorn wasteland and a bleak contrast to the gold and green of the California hills. Sometimes he yelled loudly at night. I recall opening my bedroom window and hearing his voice in the chill, damp fog. He only lived a block away yet it seemed his voice was carried on the wind for miles. Why did he yell? Who was he yelling to? I never found out. There was Whitey Whiskers who lived in a tiny cabin in an isolated canyon a mile out of town. His face was masked by a bush of white whiskers and long white hair. He dressed in old black clothes from another era and walked the mile into downtown Point Reyes to carry his groceries in a patched cloth bag. He gave us kids balloons. I remember a bright yellow one he gave me slipping out of my hand and floating high above the canyon trees, disappearing into the fog.

Next door to us in a little white house lived Philip K. Dick and his wife Kleo. Philip later became a much celebrated science fiction writer. He published 44 novels and died in 1982 when he was in his early fifties. I like this quote from his essay, "How to Build a Universe that Doesn't Fall Apart Two Days Later": "Reality is that which, when you stop believing in it, doesn't go away."

I remember when Kleo took my sister and me to the beach. Kleo was a small, dark

Point Reyes Station, 1960.

woman who had beautiful feet. Even today I have an image of her perfectly formed feet making impressions in the wet sand. Since she was Greek, perhaps in my mind, that ancestry entitled her to the physical perfection of her feet. I remember Philip as a pale, anemic man who didn't look strong, and was overweight. To a country girl like me, used to physical fitness and machismo, he looked unhealthy. Knowing looks passed between gossipy women in town when his name was mentioned. That puzzled me and I felt that those looks implied a great deal that was beyond my limited emotional knowledge. Later I realized that his life entailed high drama and sexual adventures. His nonconformist, unorthodox ideas and lifestyle were an outrage to those conventional small-town women whose highest aim was to fit in seamlessly with prevailing conventions. This was a foretaste of my education in the complexity of human beings. Years later I learned that placid appearances sometimes cover unresolved passions, secrets, and devious motives.

At home, I avoided my overly strict father and emotionally absent mother, and constructed a rich inner life with imaginary playmates. My father used cliches like "Children should be seen and not heard" as child-rearing standards. My sister and I were not allowed to speak at the dinner table or to talk when we were in the company of adults. We had lists of chores to do which were not open to negotiation. To ever

disobey his commands would insure a harsh spanking with a leather strap. He was even harsher with my mother and railed at her over the most minor violations of his orders. My sister, feistier than I, fought with him and suffered the consequences of being slapped and hit by him. I was mostly

terrified of my father's screaming rage which always
seemed unexpected and without cause. At those times
he gave little thought to what he said and was mean
and belittling. For instance, on road trips, my mother,
terrified of heights, would close her eyes and shrink
down in the car seat when we drove over steep mountain roads. My father would make fun of her and stop
the car on precipices to torture her even more.

Little wonder that my mother hid her emotional life behind a wall of vagueness and
that her sentences wandered off uncompleted as she chain-smoked cigarettes and stared
out the kitchen window hours at a time.

After World War II, prosperity was in the air and townspeople were buying new
cars in far-out colors like salmon and gray, and the first television sets. My father
insisted on buying used, pre-war cars in dark maroon and forbade us from getting
a television. When he finally bought us a television in the mid-1950s, we were only
allowed to watch two shows a week.

Part of my father's thinking had to do with making do with what one had. Buying
was a last resort. Making something oneself was better than buying it new even when
the results were dubious or worse. Cars, tractors and furniture, all repaired and liber-
ally held together with electrician's tape (the duct tape of the 1950s) were testimonials
to one's individuality and resourcefulness. Self-teaching and attempts at mastery were
applied to all situations: studying philosophy, raising goats, or even learning Greek,
which he once studied through a correspondence course. He was both arrogant and
curious.

Perhaps my father could fix anything, but not without causing damage to himself

Sketch of local buildings, 1960.

and us. The giant Stromberg Carlson radio he inherited from his sister was constantly breaking down and drove him wild with frustration and anger. Just when the Lone Ranger called out "Hi Ho Silver!" or Stella Dallas was ready to tell a dark secret, there went the radio, signaling the beginning of the next destructive repairing cycle. At first Mr. Fix-It appeared rational as he spread the inner workings of the radio on top of newspaper on the kitchen table. Slowly his jaw would set in a grimace and I knew common sense would leave soon after. Those were the days of large vacuum radio tubes and soldering irons. My mother worked the soldering iron while my sister and I held delicate bits of wire and tape in place. We never did it right, or fast enough, or held it steadily enough, and inevitably his voice would rise, yelling at us to be steady while he condemned our performance. Most of this was directed at my mother, who either pretended not to hear him or refused to answer out of passive obstinacy. I learned from those sessions that sometimes people hit with their hands, other people with their mouths, and I became aware that words have impact and can hurt.

Because of my father's capricious temperament and need for control, I avoided him as much as I could. I disliked being forced to live a life of virtuous self-deprivation and longed for more toys and later, clothes. But at the same time I was aware that the qualities of curiosity, fearlessness in the face of great odds or even reality and not caring what the neighbors thought were excellent character traits.

On the brighter side of my father's personality, he considered everything a subject for exploration. When I was five years old, he took us panning for gold at night, looking for rocks with an ultraviolet light in the heavily wooded areas of the Inverness Ridge. Never mind if you didn't succeed. The good fight was enough. He would have us sorting through rubbish bins behind department stores in Petaluma, scoring such prizes as large rolls of abandoned red paper from Christmas decorations. Near the end of his life he wanted to put his savings into an abandoned gold mine. My mother, meek as she was, for once solidly refused.

Our yard was a laboratory for self-expression. I dug large holes that went nowhere, built contraptions that had no purpose, and filled my bedroom to the ceiling with rock collections, driftwood, and broken car antennas. My father taught me how to use a hammer and nails, and I nailed together constructions that wavered between art and functional objects. I made chairs that couldn't be sat on, and I nailed together long boards into constructions that snaked around the yard. My parents just smiled and nodded their heads.

When I was 11, my father gave me some

Buckets, 1960.

paint-by-number kits. That transported me to a level of bliss I had never experienced before. I loved the smell of the oil and the turpentine, the slick way that oil paint could be mixed without drying immediately.

He saw my interest and cut wood panels for me to paint on, coating them first with a layer of white paint. This engagement with painting was an experience that was qualitatively different from other things I had done up to that point. All of my senses were alerted and I felt another dimension open for me that was surprising, yet somehow very familiar.

Painting became a logical extension of my inner and outer experiences. I could add feeling to the forms I painted and drew. At first I made pencil drawings of neighborhood houses or roses in the yard and then I filled them in with paint. I taught myself how to blend the colors but still drew in the forms first, creating my own paint-by-

Seed pods, 1960.

numbers flowers and landscapes. Gradually I let go of the pencil and simply painted what I saw around me. Each color I put on the boards seemed to have a life of its own. It was like music, but with a fullness and feeling that seemed impossible with sound.

I always felt observation was a key to success, in part because of my father's admonition that "children should be seen and not heard." So I scrutinized and examined clouds and sunsets, the quivering of leaves and the gravity of rocks. I watched the adults around me and observed the way collars enfolded necks and the expanse of textures that made up the world of fabric and skin and nylon hosiery. I loved the implied and subtle profusion of images that were left behind by the plasterers' scrapers on the ceiling of my bedroom. I entertained myself endlessly by tracing in my mind's eye the impasto forests and the elves that inhabited them.

Through my growing up years, I had very little direction from the outside world. My teachers were encouraging, enthusiastic, and helpful, but lacked art training. The only art books I could find in the library were in black and white and I had few opportunities to go to museums or galleries. I remember one exception where I received personal art instruction in a weekend watercolor class taught by a seascape painter. The teacher showed us how to paint water and sky with large brushes. My enthusiasm and sense of freedom were boundless. At last, I could see that there were people in the world who knew how to do this magic. I could learn from them.

As I grew older, I felt more freedom to explore, go to beach parties, or drive in the surrounding hills with boyfriends. I associated the heat of adolescence with the heat of the summer and the intense smells of eucalyptus and grass. Sexuality and sensuality were forever joined by the California hills.

Each day was full of small miracles. On the daily bus ride to Tomales High School, seventeen miles away, I always tried to get a window seat and spend the time on the twisty highway ride gazing out at Tomales Bay. Every day the water was a different color and mood. I spun stories to myself and saw endless images in the sky, hills, and forests.

Close to my home I had little hideaways and secret spots that I would visit daily. Each one had a different feeling to it. One was near Paper Mill Creek where deer lived. I would sit near them writing poetry or listening to the creek or the wind rattling the reeds.

All through my high school years I sat at the dining room table in the evenings, drawing endlessly on white typing paper. There I conducted experiments with drawing feelings, abstractions, and real things from my imagination. I remember deliberately opening myself to what I was feeling and allowing any emotion that I needed to express to flow on to the paper.

My artistic endeavors eventually helped me to be thought of as special by my high school teachers and peers. I painted the backdrops for school plays and helped design the high school yearbook. My talent gave me status and compensated for nameless anxieties and fears that otherwise might have overwhelmed me.

With little formal instruction available to me, I continually used my creativity as a way to express my feelings, to show my appreciation of the world, and to connect to what I felt was the great mystery of the universe. Not having structured art classes meant that I could construct what art meant to me without the limiting ideas of adults.

The combination of creativity that my father encouraged in me and the cast-iron rigidity and meanness of his child rearing in my early family life was the beginning of what I call "making a pearl from an onion." My father's parenting skills seemed to be designed to ensure his own comfort and stability and had little to do with helping his children grow emotionally. Today his limitations and willfulness in getting his own way would be likely seen as child abuse. At the time, he succeeded in having good, well-behaved children, which for my sister and me translated into feelings of deer-in-headlights terror. My mother inadvertently made the situation worse by succumbing and never saying no to him.

Throughout my life I have had to peel away distorted thinking and emotional confusion (the onion) to discover and enjoy the transcendent beauty of imagination, awe, innocence, and appreciation (the pearl) that existed within me. This contradictory home environment luckily left a part of my deepest self untrammeled, a thread of awareness and imagination that was my connection to the great conundrum of life.

I was passionate about art but I was coming up against a wall. Where could I go to learn and grow? I hungered for art training and yet I was afraid. In my small farming community I was one of the few people who cared about art. How would it be to live where others were seeking the same thing? As I graduated from high school, the forces of adolescence were pushing me out of paradise.

I knew I had to leave but didn't know how.

What next?

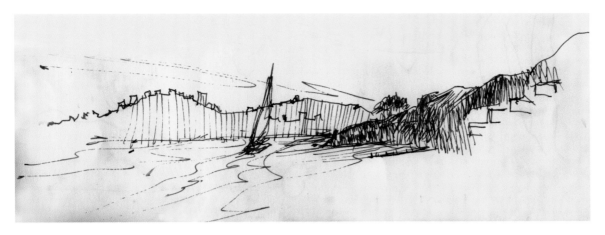

Chapter Three

After completing high school at Tomales, I attended the College of Marin in Kent-field, California, from 1960 to 1962. Even though the College of Marin was only twenty miles from Point Reyes Station, it could have been in another country. Marin County, directly north of the Golden Gate Bridge, can be roughly divided into two parts. The western part of the county is rural, agricultural, and noted for its spectacular wilderness areas. Tomales Bay and the Point Reyes Peninsula dominate it, and the creation of the Point Reyes National Seashore in the 1960s did much to retain the area's pristine qualities. East Marin was losing its agricultural roots to the suburban life that had slowly crept north of San Francisco. Though the contrast was a big one in many ways, my first step away from home allowed me to stay in contact with the land I identified with.

At the College of Marin, I came to know many of the faculty and students intimately, and I enjoyed a close-knit social community much as I had in West Marin. An added benefit was the presence of Mount Tamalpais which could be seen from most parts of the campus. Much later in life, I realized that I am most comfortable living near prominent geographic landmarks, like the sea, or mountains, as they seem a natural compass point for inner and outer positioning.

I moved from my Point Reyes Station home to an old, gray, rambling Victorian house in Ross near the college, owned by Mrs. Coddington who rented some of her rooms to college students. Mrs. Coddington, a gentle 75-year-old, had lived in the house since it was built at the turn of the century, raising her three children, and making additions to accommodate boarders. All of the furniture was nicked and worn by dogs and children, the floors were slightly slanted from years of settling, and the large high-ceilinged rooms hinted at refinement even though they hadn't been painted for decades.

Mrs. Coddington believed strongly in flying saucers and held monthly meetings in her huge living room with other saucer enthusiasts. I tiptoed up the wide stairs past the gatherings to sneak up to my room. It's not that I wasn't interested in flying saucers. It was just that I knew all I wanted to know about them at the moment. Many people in Point Reyes had seen them, including my mother, and they were an accepted part of our life in the 1950s.

In addition to Mrs. Coddington, the other permanent resident was a man named Jack, a caretaker of sorts who did odd jobs around the house and maintained the garden. Jack lived in the attic above me and nightly drank himself to sleep. I could hear the bottles hit the attic floor and roll about on the uneven boards. But somehow his drinking didn't keep him from his duties at 73 Winship Avenue and he was as easygoing as Mrs. Coddington. Together they offered me a home away from home.

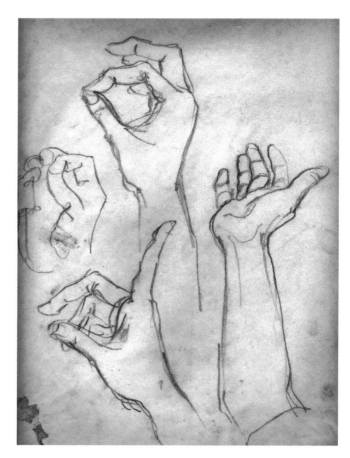

Pencil sketch, 1960.

I loved the giant old house with rambling rooms, worn furniture, and tangled gardens which, despite Jack's efforts, were unkempt and intractable—their original English formality having degenerated into a jungle of climbing plants and bushes. I had a balcony overlooking old fruit trees and flower gardens tangled with ancient vines. This was a relaxed atmosphere in which to launch a new life, and Jack and Mrs. Coddington indulged me by washing my dishes in the common kitchen and overlooking my sloppy housekeeping. I was rebuked only once by Jack for burning (yet again) a saucepan, and even then his scolding was done in a friendly manner. Though I was ashamed of myself, I seemed unable to keep things together since I put all of my energy and enthusiasm into discovering a larger world of art. I read and looked at every book in the school library. I went to every art gallery and took every art class that was offered at the college. San Francisco was only 20 miles away across the Golden Gate Bridge and whenever I could, I spent hours in its galleries and museums.

My father had always told me I could do anything I set my mind to, and he taught my sister and me how to change the oil and tires in cars, and even use a two-man chain saw. For many years, I was unconscious of the fact that women were expected to be less competent or capable than men. As a result, it never occurred to me to be daunted by equipment such as welding torches. In a beginning sculpture class, I set up the equipment in a small concrete courtyard at the college and started building a large human figure out of welding rods. I congratulated myself on how easy it was to weld. I went into the sculpture studio on weekends when no one was around and happily donned my mask and gear.

One Saturday, I went into the studio, humming to myself as I shut out the world for an hour or two. I smelled smoke. No matter, I went on welding—until I noticed flames moving up the lower part of my body. To my horror the long white smock I was wearing under the heavy apron was on fire! I turned the torch off and began fanning out the smoke and flames. I ran to the sink and put myself out. Later, exhausted from cleaning up the mess I had made, I noticed that my enthusiasm for welding had disappeared along with the fire.

I returned to drawing. I loved drawing and was good at it because I had spent so much time observing nature. This, and my enthusiasm and tenacity, compensated for my lack of know-how. All of my college art teachers encouraged me and, like Mrs. Coddington and Jack, were supportive of my creativity and passion.

One of the requirements at the College of Marin was to take an Asian art history class from Doris Meyers, a well-known local printmaker who was very outspoken and energetic. Not much older than the students, she had bluntly cut black hair and dark eyes. She was animated and verbal, and not afraid to express unpopular opinions or give enthusiastic praise. The Asian art history class, and the obvious love Doris had for Asian art, awakened me to Buddhism and the idea of contemplation as a factor in creating art. The meditative and intuitive quality of much of eastern art touched me deeply. I was fortunate to have been introduced to Asian art by Doris, who was able to transmit her experience intuitively and passionately. I remember her showing slides of the Ajanta Caves in India and feeling a great wave of recognition. For me, the incomprehensibility of life and nature were felt and contemplated before they were intellectualized. Asian art made perfect sense to me. At last I saw reflected in these art works what I had so strongly felt but couldn't put in to words: human experience is seamless and intertwined with our intellect, soul, and body; all of them having equal importance.

Doris created a lively art community outside of class, inviting students to her house for gatherings and helping to organize art events. She created an informal yet vibrant bohemian artistic circle. Through her, I met Russ Chatham, a student studying painting at the college. I was inspired by his gentle, monochromatic, contemplative scenes of West Marin. Russ was one of the first real artists I met and admired. I loved his work for its spiritual fullness and simplicity. He was only a few years older than I, yet he seemed light years more knowledgeable and confident in his art. He was to become a well-known painter of the western landscape. Russ's grandfather, Gottardo Piazzoni, who died in 1945, is still one of my favorite painters. For me, Piazzoni's soulful, intimate landscapes capture the essence of the spiritual beauty of Northern California.

Doris and Russ eventually married and they invited me to attend their wedding. At

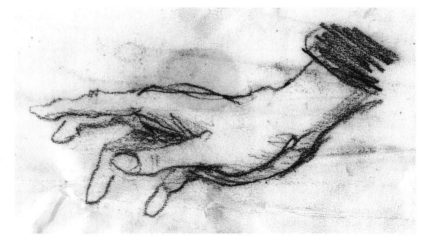

Pencil sketch, 1960.

Figure drawing ink sketches, 1961.

Gottardo Piazzoni painting murals for the San Francisco public library, 1932. Photo by Ansel Adams. © 2009 The Ansel Adams Publishing Rights Trust.

the time, they were living at the old Marconi Radio Station overlooking Tomales Bay near Marshall. The large stucco buildings built in the early 1900s hadn't been lived in for years and were overgrown with bushes and berry vines. Their ochre-colored stucco house was in a gentle state of ruin. I still remember the extraordinary beauty of the afternoon of their wedding: the startling tones of the bay unveiled by the evaporating sunlit fog. A profusion of orange monkey flowers tumbled down the cliffs towards the water. I was thrilled to be part of real artistic lives even though I was still a student.

As I absorbed each level of learning, I was pleased to be able to keep up with other students and to find myself excelling in technique and style. Since I had grown up with very little exposure to art, I was relieved to see that my lack of experience was not much of a handicap. Forty years later, I met Doris at an art opening and thanked her for her role in my artistic development. She said I was very passionate about my art and it was a pleasure to work with me. I was secretly pleased to learn that the qualities I had so admired in her were qualities I, too, was expressing.

I decided to continue my art studies at the California College of Arts and Crafts in Oakland after leaving the College of Marin. From 1962 to 1965, not only did I continue painting, but I was propelled into the maelstrom of the 1960s which was exploding politically and socially in the San Francisco Bay Area.

Chapter Four

I moved to the California College of Arts and Crafts campus in Oakland to attend school and found myself on a small urban island. Not quite in Berkeley, not quite in Oakland, the campus seemed swallowed by noisy Broadway that was next to it, an old quarry below it, a country club golf course behind it, and beyond the golf course, a cemetery. I felt that Gertrude Stein's description of Oakland, "There is no there there," summed up my response to the area. I explored Oakland on my rusty blue bike up through the hills, crisscrossing the ghetto and down past Jack London Square in the hopes of finding a geographical center for myself. But for the first time in my life I felt stranded in the geography of the place I was living in.

I felt marooned in my internal world as well; I became more introverted and increasingly ungrounded. All around me the 1960s were alive and kicking, but I was too chicken to engage in the kinds of social experimentation and exploration that my contemporaries were captivated by. I didn't understand the ramifications or consequences of my actions enough to boldly take many chances with drugs or political activism. I smoked pot and felt anything but high. Paranoia, although interesting, didn't seem like something I wanted to willingly explore in my free time. Drinking, however, was more of an enticement for me as it suited my fantasy of how a soulful bohemian artist lived. I desired very much to be a real artist, not just someone who studied art, and I was more than willing to drink myself to oblivion and party all night in the belief that I was building a significant artistic identity.

Meanwhile, the intensity and force of mid-twentieth-century art was sweeping me away in my painting classes. At this time, what was acclaimed in New York reverberated in art schools across the country and I felt the magnitude of the current movement of Abstract Expressionism in my own artistic life. Mark Rothko, Jackson Pollock, Clyfford Still, Willem de Kooning, and Robert Motherwell were among the most well-known artists of the movement. Although each of these artists had individual styles, I could relate to the monumental scale and sheer force of their paintings and to their

Facing: Checkerboard #1, 1964. Oil painting. 22" × 30". *Top:* A Warning, 1964. Oil on paper.   *25*

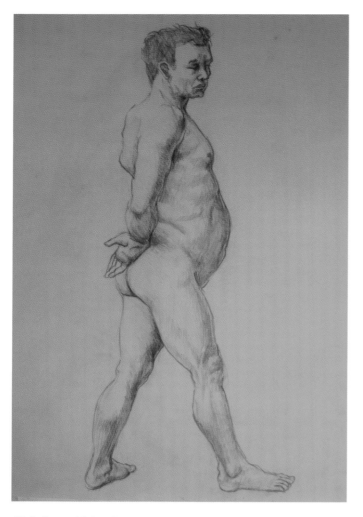

Male figure, 1963. Conté crayon.

Flo Allen, 1963. Conté crayon.

disciplined and accomplished careers. I loved most those artists that seemed to be intuitive and expressive in their work. Furthermore, I was curious and absorbed by my fellow painting students at the College of Arts and Crafts who exuberantly shared my love of art. Two of them were immensely talented and compelling artists, Dennis Oppenheim and Judy Linhares, who evolved into unconventional and unique voices in New York.

Two of my inspirations were Giorgio de Chirico and Max Ernst who employed chance and the influence of dreams to inform their work. Both of them used their technical mastery to coax intriguing and provocative imagery from the unconscious. In Surrealism, it seemed to me, the European art tradition was quirky in a way that dovetailed with the spiritual and social unrest I found in 1960s San Francisco. Much later, I was to encounter Surrealism again when I met and became friends with Julien Levy, the first art dealer in New York to exhibit the Surrealists in the late 1930s. Through him I heard firsthand reports about these artists which fleshed out my early impressions. I continually longed and

Two women, 1962. Ink on paper.

Draped figure, 1963. Conté crayon.

craved for a life that was authentic and alive versus the suburban American life that I saw as smothering yet empty.

All during the early 1960s I was in awe of the romantic, often tragic, lives of the artists, musicians, and poets I read about. I wanted to live a life outside of the constraints of what I felt was middle class and sterile. These were the years of Haight Ashbury, drugs, peace, free love, rock and roll, and flower children. For me, Janis Joplin, who I heard sing at Fillmore West, captured the fire and fanaticism of the era. Another glowing memory I have is of going with friends to the San Francisco Cow Palace and seeing Jack Kennedy speak. What enthusiasm and passion! John Wasserman, a great friend during my College of Marin days and the music and film critic for the *San Francisco Chronicle*, took me to many of these events. His ascerbic and often impertinent columns reflected the singularity of the times. In this way, popular culture came alive for me. Over time, through John I met Clint Eastwood, Ella Fitzgerald, and Joel Gray, and helped John host a party for Sammy Davis, Jr., and Maya Angelou.

At the College of Arts and Crafts, an Armenian instructor in his thirties named Sam Tchakalian became a significant influence in my life. Sam was a brilliant young abstract painter who had been born and raised in Shanghai. During the Communist takeover, he and his family were forced to give up their home and flourishing bakery business and flee China. They settled in San Francisco and Sam, after attending San Francisco State, became a painter.

Sam was mostly bald with brownish red curly hair around the edges; his most dramatic physical characteristic was his luminous dark eyes which transparently expressed whatever feelings he was experiencing. His eyes seemed to be the driving force for his stocky physique. His collaged and black oil paintings were the extension and expression of his life force. His paintings, stark yet lush, opened up intuitive deep space and communicated highly charged and enigmatic spiritedness. Some of the pieces were small, but the most startling work he did was large and monumental. The collage component imparted a three dimensional effect, and the black oil paint he used deepened and stirred the paintings into expressive passion. In his work, I felt some of the mysterious affinity with the unconscious that had interested me in Asian art and early

Sam Tchakalian at Sea Cliff, San Francisco, 1964.

Surrealism. Since Sam was raised in Shanghai, it made sense that he had an affinity for Asian spiritual beliefs.

When he taught he used passionate action words, with curses and expletives popping like champagne corks. "Goddamn it! Move it. . . . get rid of it. . . . That's it!" He was constantly in motion. As a teacher he transferred to students the fire he felt as a painter and the importance of the artist's life. For many decades, he inspired students with his spontaneous teaching style. Sam loved painting more than anything in the world and was able to transmit a mixture of spirituality and physicality that was soulful and relevant. He didn't just teach Abstract Expressionism, he communicated the very essence of the painter's soul and the complete joy it imparted.

Up to this point in my creative life, my natural instinct had kept me from intellectualizing my artistic process, but Sam was the first teacher that inspired me to truly trust my intuition and passion. Knowing him also helped me to channel my inner turmoil and bafflement with the 1960s into the constructive outlet of artistic expression. I felt I had an anchor in the briny deep.

Like many of his male contemporaries in the art world, he dressed in bland gray sport jackets, button-down shirts, and plain brown shoes. But there his conformity to mainstream lifestyle ended. He lived and worked in a ramshackle warehouse in the Mission District of San Francisco under a freeway on-ramp to Highway 101. Here he stayed until the end of his life in 2004 with nothing more than the rudiments of plumbing and homemaking paraphernalia. Unlike other artists who may have started out living in poverty but later in their lives grew to cherish the trappings of expressive or expensive lifestyles, Sam kept his warehouse space with the same bare beams, rough floors, and used furniture that he started with. He drove cheap, old, broken-down cars from the 1950s way too fast, not out of quirky taste as much as they suited his needs of transporting paintings. Also, they looked like him: menacing, out of date, unapologetic.

For Sam, staying true to his real self meant he was not to be a commercial success. He seemed to consciously cultivate a social self that was often obnoxious and uncompromising in order to not pander to what was commercially popular. He vigorously protected his artistic freedom even when it wasn't in the best interest of his career.

In his mind, artistic freedom meant living on the edge. He took me to smoky poolrooms at 2 a.m. in Chinatown. He was a brilliant pool and snooker player who intimidated his opponents as much with physical menace as with his finely-tuned skills. Living on the edge also included intense partying and gambling. For instance, I rode with Sam when he was driving with his car lights off on railroad tracks near Peter Voulkos's studio after one of Peter's popular parties in Berkeley. Peter, celebrated on the West Coast for his bronzes and clay pieces, was a riveting magnet in the San Francisco art world at that time. There I met Elaine de Kooning, Ray Parker, and others from the New York art world. I envisioned New York as a more supportive scene than San Francisco. From what I heard about New York, a lively and diverse artist population existed there that could sustain both living needs and the strength of one's convictions. Fact or fiction, this image was tantalizing and I could feel myself being drawn to New York.

Decades later, a former student of Sam's met me and told me she was puzzled by something he said about me. She had mentioned my name in passing to him and he had

Black and White Abstract, 1964. Oil on paper. 22" × 30".

Checkerboard #4, 1964. Oil on paper. 22" × 30".

said in reply, "Susan Hall was so small, a rat could eat her, hat and all." I laughed out loud. This was a rhyme that he had teased me with years earlier.

During this time, I attempted to understand observations about the artistic life that would trouble me for decades. For one thing, I could see that competition in the outer art world could be detrimental to the integrity of the self and soul I had wrestled so long with. Many artists depended on galleries to show their work and wealthy collectors to purchase it. Since there were not that many galleries or collectors, a natural human tendency to excel and be successful could result in competition to be part of that system. Almost unconsciously, voices and opinions could pressure an artist to be more outer-directed than inner-directed. Forces of the market could take precedence over the voice of the spirit. I was confused by the feelings this observation generated in me. I felt that striving for excellence and perfection might compromise telling the truth of my own life. I was unsure how my need for inner exploration could fit in with the outer world of the 1960s.

Then again, I was disoriented as my self-assurance and confidence as a woman began to break down. Athough many of the best art students were women, very few women were teachers. Even fewer were showing their work or being written about. I didn't yet have words for the disparity I saw and experienced, but I knew at some

level that it was frustrating and painful
to me.

I was disheartened that the expression of feelings in painting was gen-
erally belittled and that the intellect
seemed to be paramount. Critical
thinking was foremost, it seemed, in
developing as an artist. My own experience of emotions seemed to me to be
the most important thing in my life as
an artist. After all, feelings are the primary response to being alive and the
drive of the self towards expression.
I didn't want to sacrifice the directness
and spontaneity I felt as an untrained
artist by deadening my responses with
academic training. I was a disciplined
artist, yes, but I drew and painted
skillfully in order to express my awe
of life and being alive.

To further confuse me and pull me
in different directions, many of my
teachers encouraged me to paint monu-
mental paintings which felt distant
and cold to me. I preferred the intimacy and warmth of small canvases
which expressed my inwardness.
I vacillated between feeling loss at
what I had experienced growing up
in West Marin and the earnest desire
to continue growing. At time the gains
I made seemed dubious.

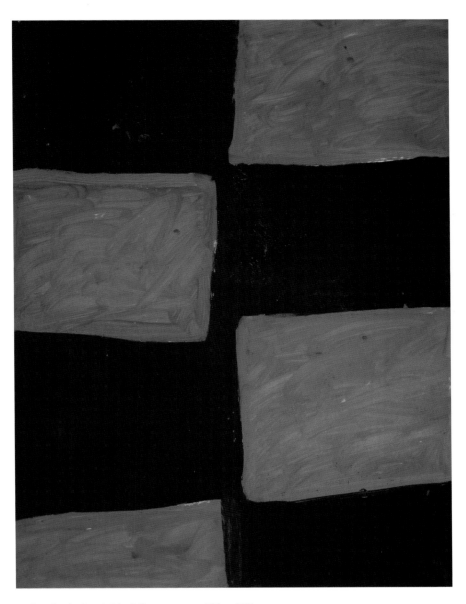

Red and Black, 1964. Oil on paper. 22" × 30".

As I look back, the jumble of emotions I felt take on some clarity: now I can see
that I wanted clear answers and not ambiguity. In hindsight, I realize that growing
isn't a matter of finding clear solutions, but of living with the discomfort of the search.
Though these same issues still challenge me today, I now know that questioning itself
opens up an inner spaciousness. This, I've found, is what is truly satisfying to me. The
process is a little like living in a home that in time becomes too small, old, or uncomfortable. Then begins the process of renovating and tearing down walls to make room
for expansion. Each transition to a new renovation of self and individuality implies
letting go of what one is currently living with.

What I realized over the years is that identities are bridges for the self to expand and
not a stopping place. I sensed that living from the inside out and knowing oneself first
was more important than expecting the outside world to give me identity. This has been
a lifelong journey for me and has entailed much insecurity and questioning. Dealing
with insecurity and a lack of moorings pushed me in one direction and then another,
but my self-identity, however frail, endured and expanded.

Chapter Five

From 1965–67, I attended the Master of Art program at the University of California, Berkeley. In the last semester of my studies, I enrolled in an advanced painting seminar class taught by Mark Rothko, who was visiting the campus for a semester. Even then, Rothko was acknowledged as a master painter of Abstract Expressionism. He was revered in the art world for the depth and brilliance of his work. His paintings had a strong wordless, contemplative, and spiritual aspect. Coupled with a painting style that was forthright and simple, his work was highly respected and admired.

Mark was an unassuming man, who wore glasses and was balding. Like my other male painting teachers (and they were almost all male) he wore the nondescript sports coats, pants, and button-down shirts of the previous era. The flamboyant look of the hippie generation didn't arrive until much later.

In fact, if I didn't know that Mark was an artist, and a famous one at that, there would be little to identify him as such. I remember his hands trembling; was he ill? I didn't know, and since I was so young, age itself seemed like an illness. He was very candid about his professional life in our class; in one session he discussed his fame and how uneasily it sat on his shoulders. The artists of his time in New York had very little commercial support and for the most part were extremely poor, which is why most of them taught or lived irregular lives. In fact, the lives that artists were able to cobble together were a badge of honor. When collectors and museums and galleries began to show interest in the Abstract Expressionists, the effect was as disruptive as it was positive. The components that had created their identity were suddenly in disarray. Many found in alcohol a way to help them through and to keep on with a bohemian lifestyle. Commercialism was an uncomfortable counterpart to the strong, passionate ideals that many of these artists possessed.

Each week, Mark met with the graduate students to critique their work. At the end of the semester he planned on visiting each of us in our studio. I was nervous about him coming to my studio and I put great effort into having the paintings I wanted

Top facing: 725 Greenwich Street, San Francisco; *below facing*: The Alley, via Buffano, side entrance. Top: Roof garden, 725 Greenwich Street.

55

Building canvas stretchers.

him to look at presented properly. My studio in San Francisco's North Beach was the quintessential 1960s artist's loft. It was part of an old horse stable that had been turned into an appliance warehouse. The top part, where I lived and worked, was rickety, run down and unpainted. In many places, the sky could be seen through the weathered siding. The entire first floor, about two thousand square feet, was filled with refrigerators and stoves, some old and worn out, others new, still in their boxes. From my front windows upstairs I could see San Francisco Bay and Alcatraz Island, and at night, a fog light swept across my windows. Intrusive, perhaps, but also it seemed to say, "I am here, I am here," making the atmosphere in my studio feel protective. I particularly loved the sound of the foghorn which was very low pitched and rumbled underneath the fog.

From the roof, where I built a garden and eating area, I could see the steep incline of North Beach and Russian Hill. I often sat out there whether it was foggy or windy, relishing the aromas from the Italian coffeehouses, cheese stores and tiny vegetable and fruit stands that dotted the Washington Square area. My studio was dilapidated, but to me it was a wondrous constellation in my artistic sky. During this time I shared my archaic home with an artist girlfriend who was finding more fulfillment as a popular topless exotic dancer on nearby Broadway. I loved visiting her (Naja was her stage name) in the sleazy nightclub where she danced. I was fascinated by the imaginative melodrama that unfolded backstage and spent time drawing one of the dancers who was also a contortionist.

In preparation for the Rothko visit, I set my paintings against the large wall that divided the room in two. I made Mark tea in the living area and brought it to him at a worktable by the windows. I was as nervous about making tea for him as showing him my work. Anything related to cooking was as foreign to me as space travel and to this day, I struggle with my aversion to pots, pans, and the whistle of a kettle. We sipped our tea quietly. When we were done, I turned over the canvases that were stacked against the wall so he could look at them. I didn't know what to expect. Would he be critical? Would he tell me to stop painting? I'd had a teacher who told me outright I had no talent and others who intimated that I'd be better off doing something else.

When Mark spoke about my work, he was supportive, encouraging, and kind. He asked me to turn over each painting until they were in a line so that the whole body of my work could be seen at once. Although he may have used some of the current Abstract Expressionist terms to talk about what I was painting, he spoke naturally, without pretense, and was attentive and cordial. In fact, he put me more at ease than

Mark Rothko and his painting *No. 15 (White, Red, on Yellow)*. Mixed media on canvas. 95⅜" × 81⅜".
Images copyright © The Metropolitan Museum of Art / Art Resource, NY.

I had ever felt with any of my teachers. His quiet manner put me on an equal footing
with him, someone who was working and struggling with the same issues. He was
unhurried and calm, looking me in the eyes as he spoke. He created a simple, direct
human connection with me not only as an artist, but as a person.

He asked me questions about my work. He did not linger on individual paintings but
was more interested in my overall process. At one point he told me that the surface of
my paintings was "activated." By this I mean that a major concern in modern art since
Cubism was creating a dynamic picture plane surface. Two-dimensional space was
to have as much power to convey meaning and dimension as the illusion of three-
dimensional space had in European art of the past. This meant that the modern artist
painted directly and was not so concerned with the conjuring of the illusion of another
world outside the canvas. The word "activated" was not a term that I was familiar with
so it challenged me to think in a different way about my painting.

This visit had a subtle and profound effect on me. It was a validating experience for
me as an artist. It took me many years to realize that this visit planted a seed of self-
esteem in my imagination that allowed me to take myself seriously.

Without making a conscious decision, in the next weeks I stopped painting and
cleared out, threw out everything in my studio including paint, art works, portfolios
of drawings, and half-finished canvases. Gone, gone, gone! I painted the walls bright
white and covered the old paint smears and marks.

I sat in a folding chair in the middle of the studio and hugged its emptiness. The
wonderful freshness of the wind and fog swept through my open windows and I reveled
in the beauty of this simple, empty place. After some time had passed, I felt an urge
to put up a small table in the middle of the room. I put a folding chair next to the
table and on the table I placed a single sheet of paper and a pencil. Every day I came
into my studio and sat at the table for a period of time, never for more than an hour.

Abstract #5, 1965. Acrylic on paper. 22" × 30".

In these early experiments it was more likely half an hour. Finally I shortened the sessions to as little as five or ten minutes.

It could be said that my first objective was to listen to myself as respectfully as I had been listened to by Mark Rothko. First I turned off the radio and telephone. Then I sat quietly at my table not controlling my thoughts or feelings. I heard the squealing of cable car brakes outside; I felt the sharp bursts of wind coming from the San Francisco Bay ruffling my sleeves and turning the edges of the paper on the table. Thoughts came and went, some grabbing my attention. Whatever went on, I just sat quietly, my hand with a pencil in it but drawing nothing.

By quieting my surroundings and my own body, I felt the sensate experience of the present moment. I was surprised that it was so simple and, for me, so quiet, so unpretentious. "This awareness of the present moment would be very easy to miss," I said to myself. It was not a big deal, startling, or particularly significant.

After sitting for awhile, I noticed a desire to draw. I began to scribble and observed how I responded and felt as I scribbled. After some minutes, I became fascinated with what appeared as the beginning of a drawing of a shape, a box or a table. This was so intriguing to me I completely forgot that I was drawing at all and became totally engrossed with the drawing of the table. Before I knew it, the half hour had passed. I stopped drawing and turned the paper over so I couldn't see what I had been doing.

This procedure continued for a few more sessions. After I became familiar with the process, I became aware that I could create some guidelines that would help me to move along in the investigation of my artistic process.

Here are some of the things that I felt were important:

It is important to: ✎

1. Set up an area that is quiet and without distractions.
I cleared out my studio and asked myself what objects and artwork I wanted in it.
In my case, I cleaned everything out and put a simple table in the middle of the room.

2. Have the drawing area prepared beforehand. Start the first session with a large sheet of white paper and a pencil.
I found the less thinking or planning I did, the better. If I had everything set up I could draw and not spend my time cleaning off a space, or finding ways to procrastinate, like sharpening pencils.

3. Sit quietly for a few minutes, pencil in hand, letting everything settle down before beginning; allow an attitude of listening and observing to be foremost.
By quieting my surroundings and even my own body, I could begin to focus on the present moment that was essentially mine. This was neither an abstraction, nor an idea, but something felt in my body and expressed on paper. It was the opposite of the way I had approached my painting and drawing in the past. I'd always had a specific goal or plan in mind. When I decided to not have a specific objective in mind, my drawing was unthinking, spontaneous, and completely undirected.

4. Have some sort of timer to indicate the ending of the session. At first, set it for five minutes. After doing this process for some time, say two weeks, lengthen the time to 10 minutes.
Having a timer meant that I would have a short time limit that didn't depend on my decision to stop or continue. This time constraint helped focus the session and relieved me from having to craft or plan a work of art or even have an opinion.

5. Once beginning to draw, continue and don't stop until the end of the session. Movement, not evaluation, is crucial to this practice.
Stopping seems to invite assessment, judgment, criticism, analysis, and the desire to improve on the drawing.
   I felt free to do nothing but scribble if no direction presented itself. A straight line or a curved line was good enough. When physical discomfort arose (which was often) or my mind shouted endless ideas and strategies for making a good drawing, I could thumb my nose at them, take a deep breath, and continue moving my pencil. I made allowance for this chatter and continued drawing.

6. If thoughts or feelings are overwhelming, or if there is a desire to stop before the session ends, take a breath and continue drawing even if there is nothing but scribbles.
Again, **movement, not evaluation** was the most important reality. Slowly, I began to trust the process of what I was doing.

7. Turn the drawing over or put it aside for at least a couple of weeks, suspend judgment.
Once again, I suspended judgment and postponed any desire to judge or make good art. This was about my own "beingness" as I made art, not intellect. Over time this new awareness grew into self-respect and a luminous self-honoring.

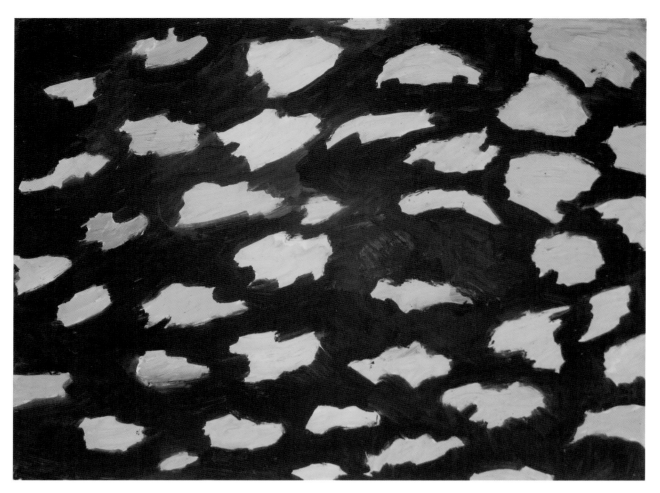

Abstraction #4, 1965. Oil on paper. 22" × 30".

Abstraction #5, 1965. Oil on paper. 22" × 30".

What gradually evolved was a direction that surprised me. These simple drawings and scribblings expanded into figures. They evolved into drawings of women doing simple things—standing, looking. Although poorly drawn, they had an unpretentiousness that was quietly energetic. Before I knew it, my abstract art developed into narrative art, which was metaphorical, symbolic, ironic. My art became fresh and alive to me.

If I were to describe my artistic abilities as a river, I would say: before these experiments I was hacking away at a channel that was blocked, forcing it to go where I wanted it to go. I used the techniques I learned in school and relied on the Art World and Art History for ideas about art and becoming an artist, but I knew something was missing.

Now I was relaxed. I followed the river channel that was opening for me. The difference was startling. I felt connected in a very subtle but sure way. I felt this new direction was supportive yet fluid. It stimulated my imagination and sustained me. Making art was exciting and fulfilling.

In time, my work became more complex, but somehow it didn't matter so much what it looked like as long as I was caught in the current of my creative river. I began to recognize certain qualities of this creative flow. Even though I couldn't force them to come to me, I could shift my awareness to them when I recognized their presence.

Some of these qualities were a sense of effortlessness and of being in the flow. I felt generous in allowing everything to happen as it wished. All of my faculties were present but none dominated. I let the flowing feeling direct me. Relaxation and alertness were essential. I had the sensation of paying attention to what I was doing, not what I was thinking.

I found after awhile that I could recognize this state, with its body and mind sensations. If nothing occurred when I sat down to work, I couldn't force it or conjure it. A certain quiet patience, recognition, and respect were necessary. It was like sailing and finding oneself becalmed, and then recognizing the barest hint of a breeze and responding to it. The energy I gained from this process was inspiring.

I was exhilarated to be an artist.

movement not evaluation

Chapter Six

I planned to visit New York in the summer of 1969. A sign of my naivete as I had no concept of how muggy and humid New York summers are.

I could hardly afford such a trip. After graduation from Berkeley I had been teaching painting and drawing in the University of California Art Department so I had a regular salary. To supplement that I, like so many other young people in the 1960s, seasonally worked at the post office. I needed to earn more money, so in the summer of 1968, I began to increase my hours there. It never occurred to me to ask for financial help from my parents. They had contributed to my undergraduate schooling and I didn't ask for financial support after that. All through school I held part-time jobs such as being a waitress, a telephone operator, and working for the university.

My position at the post office near the Port of San Francisco was the one I held the longest. I was there to help the customs inspector open crates and boxes from Asian freighters and inspect them for illegal substances. I loved it! I got a great physical workout lifting boxes and crates off the conveyor belt for the inspector and I enjoyed the thrill of opening foreign packages that weren't mine. According to post office mythology, the previous person in my job had eaten some cookies in one of the crates and never returned.

Finally, in the summer of 1969, I made my first visit to New York City. My boyfriend at the time, Edward Scher, an art student in his early 20s, was also enthusiastic about going to New York. A mutual friend had moved to the West Village and invited us to stay with her. I had read about its historic and colorful history, which reminded me of North Beach in San Francisco. My conceptions of New York City were vague notions, mostly myth, with a few half-baked facts thrown in. At last I would see New York City with my own eyes.

The only landmark I could identify from the taxi was the Chrysler Building in midtown Manhattan. I knew that Manhattan was an island surrounded by water but I only saw tiny sightings of open spaces in the midst of cement. Edward and I reached an imposing, anonymous brick apartment building on Hudson Street. Despite the somber and seemingly impenetrable solidity of the building, our friend's tiny apartment on the fourth floor didn't appear to have any protection at all from the external world and did little to filter the sounds of the city.

Not only did every taxi, car, and truck on Hudson Street honk its horn constantly, but it also seemed that all were equipped with wooden wheels, more square than round —rattling and jolting on the cobblestones. Could anyone make a move in New York City without screaming or honking? This din was accompanied by the throbbing and shaking from the underground subway system. My brain was red-alerting the rest of me that I was in big trouble.

Nothing in my consciousness from my heretofore bucolic life would make any sense at all here. I found myself tripping off curbs, falling on stairs, banging into doors, dodging delivery vans. I overreacted to careening taxis when the real danger was that open manhole on the corner which I missed only by acrobatics.

I was thrilled, awed, and horrified. Seeing Rembrandt's paintings in the Metropolitan Museum of Art nearly brought me to my knees. This is what art is capable of doing, I thought. The sum total of the paintings triggered responses I had only felt while meditating or reading great poetry or listening to music. Matisse and Monet in the Museum of Modern Art lifted me to transcendent ecstasy. In their work, the brilliance of color was the vehicle which brought me joy. Despite these rarified experiences, later, in the street, I found myself narrowly missing a poorly aimed stream of spit or being dragged into the undertow of crowds so thick I couldn't see daylight.

Edward and I arranged to meet a UC classmate named Carol who lived in the Bronx and taught at a local community college. She explained it was much cheaper to live there. We three dawdled over a late pasta lunch in the Village and then Carol insisted that she "show us" the Bronx, though I didn't know what she had in mind. "You don't have to live in Manhattan," she persisted as we rode uptown in a local subway to 42nd Street where, she explained, we'd transfer to an express. "Be there in no time."

The express arrived: I saw a massive blur of people. They piled out of the train, others piled aboard, rush-rush, hurry-hurry, breathless motion. Then the express roared away. It vanished into a dark tunnel. With it went Ed and Carol.

I was left standing alone, on the platform.

Later Edward told me, "We didn't know what to do, we didn't know what you'd do." This was decades before cell phones. Carol was hysterical. "Oh my God," she kept repeating to him, "I thought she was with you!"

Amazingly, I simply jumped on the next express train, not having any idea where it was going, but I stayed on until the end of the line. It seemed like a safe thing to do. When I "surfaced," it was dusk and I was in a foreign country. The craggy landscape was dominated by shabby two-story buildings, falling-apart row houses, jagged garbage-strewn sidewalks, bawling babies, and heavyset mothers who babbled no language known to me.

I'd survived the belly of the beast, that is, the subway, but now what? There wasn't a phone booth in sight. I squared my shoulders and walked purposefully down the street saying to myself, "You're all right, you're invisible, don't be afraid." Scruffy teenage boys, huddled on a stoop stared at me, but, of course they didn't see me. How could they? I was just a 25-year-old blonde with a great figure and a sun-kissed California tan, wearing a mini-skirt that was fond of blowing into my face if the wind came up. Like I said, I was invisible. Did one of the teens whistle or was that screechy noise in my head?

Soon I passed a kind of storefront where guys of various shapes and sizes sat at desks behind a glass window talking into telephones. "Buenos días," I tried, rolling out high school Spanish. "Hey, where am I?" "The South Bronx, whatcha think? Las Vegas?" Luckily I was at a gypsy cab company. The drivers couldn't have been friendlier.

A cheery Cuban whose wife sat in a corner drinking beer offered to take me where I was going but I didn't know where I was going. I emptied my entire purse and found Carol's number on a scrap of paper. Carol paid the driver when I arrived at her apartment.

It was my first and last trip to the Bronx.

Hygeia Sipper Has a Smoke, 1969. Acrylic on canvas. 40" × 36".

Chapter Seven

The experiences I had on this eight-day trip did not dampen my enthusiasm. I focused on the unclear, yet powerful feeling that New York was where I belonged. My aesthetic and spiritual experiences in galleries and museums, and with the artists that I met were exhilarating. New York was where I could continue a great artistic quest.

I learned that composer-musician Terry Riley, who was living in New York City, wanted to move to San Francisco. His albums, *In C* and *Rainbow in Curved Air* are still among my favorites. He was then in the forefront of American avant-garde music. (I have remained in touch with the outstanding pianist Katrina Krimsky, who is one of Terry's close friends and fellow musicians.) Would I be interested in trading my studio in San Francisco for his in New York City? The rents were close enough—my studio was seventy-five dollars a month and Terry's was ninety dollars. Edward and I figured that by early 1970 we could save enough money to live in New York for six months without working.

Edward and I took a red-eye flight and arrived back in New York in the early hours of a bleak January morning in 1970. This time the temperature was six degrees above zero. Snow and ice blotched the streets. As our taxi crossed Bowery and Houston, we saw homeless men, hands outstretched, warming themselves at a fire in an oil drum. The bleakness increased when we entered Terry's place on Bowery and Grand Street. Today this area, sort-of SoHo, is gentrified with posh boutiques. In those days it was for Bowery bums—and worse. I had traded my light and airy San Francisco loft overlooking the dazzling San Francisco Bay for this dark, dilapidated "apartment."

Although we had two stories of living space, with wide floorboards and a fireplace, we were knocked sideways by the broken windows, low uneven ceilings, and claustrophobically small, airless rooms. Smells from the luncheonette downstairs wafted upstairs, leaving behind the greasy aroma of stale hamburgers and French fries. Gina's

Clockwise from upper left: 246 Grand Street, home sweet home, above Gina's bridal shop; nearby Orchard Street; brides across the street; a neighbor.

Tessie's Gowns, next door.

Bridal Shop was on the second floor and Gina was always screeching in Italian at her seamstresses.

My "studio" was in the room with our bathtub; the rest of the plumbing was up two flights. I covered the tub with a board when I painted. The only window and light source in that tiny room was masked with a massive steel grate. Five feet behind this burglar deterrent was a dirty gray building. Despite the grimness of the apartment, I was determined to focus on my work. Six months of savings hitched me to my dreams. This is where I created large acrylic paintings on canvas.

My artistic output was helped by my practice of Transcendental Meditation, popular then in San Francisco. My spiritual clarity was deeply affected by this practice and it provided a level of relaxation and integration that was sustaining. I could feel a sense of tranquility that wasn't disturbed by my thoughts. I was able to dispel much of my inner turmoil and maintain some stability in the midst of overstimulation. As I extended my social spheres in the art world, I realized there was a tremendous amount of social pressure to join in drinking and drugs. I was able to resist because of my meditation practice, and socializing with other meditators fortified my stance.

After six months of painting diligently, I had a decent body of work and was feeling the pull to show it to other artists and gallery dealers. Walter De Maria, a friend of Terry's and mine, generously introduced me to Holly Solomon, a well-known Pop Art patron who was then buying the work of young artists. She bought some of my paintings and enthusiastically introduced me to other wealthy art patrons who also purchased my paintings.

Holly said that she loved the personal, intimate connection I had within my art and the fact that I painted so many female figures. Her salons at her apartment on East 57th Street and in her Greene Street loft overflowed with writers, poets and painters. Over a drink and an avocado dip at the Lower Manhattan Ocean Club I was soon talking to Marcia Tucker, one of the curators from the Whitney Museum. Later, after a studio visit, Marcia offered me an exhibition at the museum in January 1972.

I had painted all of the Whitney canvases in the tiny dark bathtub room with a minimum of paint and a couple of small brushes. The room was so small I couldn't get more than a few feet away from anything I was working on. So I was shocked and amazed when I finally saw the show installed at the Whitney. It was the first time I had seen

The Architect, 1972. Acrylic on canvas. 63" × 63". Private collection.

Projection, 1970. Acrylic on canvas. 60" × 62". Private collection.

the whole body of work together. I could stand in the center of the room and for the first time see each painting from a distance.

The exhibition was powerful. This body of narrative work consisted of pale grounds painted with thin, vulnerable outlines of figures, exclusively women, in various situations and environments. The paintings paralleled my life experience; how I saw myself in the world, my vision of the richness of life, my experience as a woman. Much of the work echoed and commented on the Women's Movement. It revealed the dilemmas of women regarding fashion, men's view of them, and self image. This was the beginning of the Women's Movement and a deep sea change was taking place in how women viewed themselves.

The paintings were of women in life situations such as architects, businesswomen, and waitresses. For instance, a painting called *The Waves*, painted in sinuous, slender outlines, depicted solitary women in boats on the open sea. Pale washes barely covered the canvases. The effect was subtle because it wasn't until the viewer was very close that the entire image could be seen. From a distance, the paintings

Holly Solomon at 246 Grand Street, 1971.

gave a feeling of intangible visual intensity which clarified and increased as one approached the image.

My paintings of female figures were sensitive, limpid; painted in translucent pastel colors. I had always been good at drawing and the pale forms were constructed with strong compositions. They were beautiful and personal. More often than not, the women were nude, covered by transparent clothing. I hesitate to analyze them intellectually, because for me they were sensual, mythical, and imaginative statements. The eyes were blank, much like early archaic Greek figures. I didn't imitate these dignified archetypal forms, but only discovered later on that I had painted facets of these historic and grounded figures.

Often my paintings of women portrayed them with large feet and legs that were firmly planted in their situations and lives. These were not feminist rebels, but stoic women; humor and wit upheld them. They were strong; unafraid to show who they were through their transparent clothing. I was so young and exuberant that the darker dramas women and other societal underdogs struggled with were not foremost in my mind.

Opening at 57th Street, 1971.

Horace Solomon, Holly Solomon, and
Leo Castelli, 1971.

My early encouragement came from
a father who told me I could do anything. He was consciously supportive of
my artistic endeavors and also adamant
about teaching my sister and me sur-
vival skills. He taught my sister Morse
code (I guess he worried one day she
might be stranded in a small, handmade
sailing craft stranded in the South Seas)
and both of us were skilled with axes for
chopping wood or building fences. Perhaps he inspired these strong yet delicate
females?

I remember walking past the Whitney when my show was up and seeing
my name on the outside of the building.
I didn't feel as if I had conquered New
York, but I did feel an acknowledgment
of my existence since I could see my
name prominently displayed in a highly
respected place. The attention and
publicity I received transported me into
a wider artistic world. Yet, at the same
time, I was puzzled about the meaning
of this event and didn't know what effect
it would have on my life.

Horace Solomon in his office with a Cy Twombly painting, 1971.

Chapter Eight

Daily life in New York was still difficult. The Bowery-Little Italy neighborhood where we lived was dangerous. Our apartment had been broken into twice. The first burglar jimmied the iron grate on the back window of our bedroom and relieved us of many of our San Francisco belongings including valuable stereo equipment, a TV, cameras; in short, anything that brought pleasure to our lives.

After that first robbery we acquired a dog, Benjamin, a coon hound and Doberman mix, who was an abused stray proficient in canine attack training. Benjamin was a perfect match for the maltreated, periodically aggressive Burmese cat named Wingtree that we also took in. Benjamin's best feature was a bark from hell. His worst feature was that he hated Italian men (unfortunately we lived in Little Italy) and would lunge barking and slobbering at them any time I took him out for walks, whether three in the morning or afternoon.

I made myself ready for danger in the home or on the streets. Physically, I was strong, could run fast, and I slowly developed street smarts. I no longer took for granted that my home was safe. Now, I always paused after entering the front door, quieting myself to see if I sensed any intrusion, and I never entered a room if I couldn't turn on the light from the doorway. On the sidewalk, particularly at night, when I was without Benjamin, I walked close to the street. I developed peripheral vision so I was aware of what was around me at all times. I was better than Dick Tracy!

With this rigorous self training I foiled the next burglar. One afternoon as I entered our apartment, I saw the shadow of a man fumbling at the corner of the opaque glass of the skylight between our bedroom and the living area. I saw sky for the first time coming through the roof as the skylight edge was pried open with a crowbar. Shocked, I stood transfixed as the side was slowly rising and sky and wind filled the entryway. Finally, I shouted Benjamin's attack commands. He obeyed, but raced towards the front door, slavering and yowling at the mailbox! I was furious and screamed so loudly, that I scared off the intruder. The skylight was dropped, dirt and dust filled the air, and

Top facing: *Fan mail*, 1972. Acrylic on canvas. 18" × 24". Private collection.
Below facing: *Room with a View*, 1972. Acrylic on canvas. 18" × 24". Private collection.
Top: Hosiery display.

The Glove Display, 1972. Acrylic on canvas. 24" × 17". Private collection.

I saw the moving shadow of the burglar's foot as he ran off the roof.

Despite the burglaries, this teeming multicultural neighborhood was a fairly protected place. The heart of Little Italy, a few blocks away, was kept safe by the Mafia (unless you were unlucky enough to be in Umberto's Clam House the night Joey Gallo was murdered there). The Chinese in Chinatown were family-centered and the Chinese drug gangs of the '80s and '90s did not yet exist. The Hasidim kept to themselves on the other side of the Bowery and did not interact much with outsiders. The one faction that could be unpredictable was the Bowery grifters that skulked in the side streets.

There were many flop houses along with a spillover of homeless street people. Many were alcoholics or addicts sometimes suffering from dementia or delirium tremens and their psychotic behavior gave a sense of madness to the Bowery, day or night. The artists and musicians who lived amidst this cacophony rented the cheap and fairly plentiful apartments and lofts. They were a poor and benign group aspiring to fulfill their destinies as creative people. I was inspired and encouraged by this artistic community.

This loosely connected society was centered in the grim grid of nineteenth-century cast-iron buildings below Houston Street, over to the Bowery and bordered by Chinatown. Artists scrounged out living space in lofts between marginal factories and commercial enterprises. These were the pre-SoHo, pre-Tribeca days; and rag merchants and warehouses still occupied most of the lofts below Houston Street. Most buildings were multi-storied walkups; only a few of the larger ones had old freight elevators.

Young impoverished artists could find inexpensive lofts in these neighborhoods. I looked at a second-story space on the Bowery that had once been Mark Rothko's studio. It had been a men's club in the late 1900s when the Bowery thrived with theatres and vaudeville houses. Two giant stone fireplaces sat at each end of the room and it had wonderfully high ceilings. But $110 a month was too expensive. I didn't even think about moving there.

In the early 1970s the community of New York artists, museum curators, and collectors was small, so it was impossible not to know almost everyone at least superficially, from Robert Rauschenberg to the most recent hopeful art student.

I felt comfortable in this loose-knit and supportive community. The Women's Movement was burgeoning into a formidable voice that was penetrating the art world. The writer Lucy Lippard was one of the first champions of women artists in this new era, and was instrumental in organizing and writing about this artistic unfolding. A fiery intellectual who vibrated with great energy, she was always interested and available for conversation whenever I saw her on West Broadway or in a women's gathering. She organized a groundbreaking show at the Aldrich Museum in Ridgefield, Connecticut, titled *26 Contemporary Women Artists*. Artists of the caliber of Jackie Winsor, Mary Heilmann, Alice Aycock, and Cynthia Carlson were included in the exhibition. Lucy also put together a book of essays by women artists entitled *Finding Her Center*, in which I was included.

For the first time in Western art history, entire exhibitions were devoted to women. Marcia Tucker, another great crusader for women's art, spotlighted women in her curatorial work at the Whitney. She put 100% of her energy into the movement.

The Sculpture Garden, 1972. Acrylic on canvas. 18" × 18". Private collection.

Marcia had a great sense of humor and I remember rollicking dinner parties at her loft in the mid-twenties of Manhattan where I laughed so hard I thought I would endanger my health. One night we sang country western songs we made up. The best part of mine was the title, "She Melted my Heart in the Frying Pan of Love." I couldn't sing, was tone deaf, and couldn't come up with more than one line so I was quickly over-shadowed by Dave Hickey, who was a bona fide wordsmith and raconteur. Another time, I remember Marcia dressing as a lower East Side Hassidim at a costume party complete with a black-rimmed felt hat and side locks. Since she was a good actress, she could carry off serious intensity and solemnity without saying a word. Her pale skin and dark eyes gave her an air of severe rabbinical authority.

These and many other women were instrumental in forming women's groups that addressed specific issues such as social and economic equality. They wrote in art journals and curated shows. Many other heroic women challenged the male-dominated art world and launched the Women's Movement in art. What equality exists in the art world today is a direct result of these efforts. Women began to take themselves seriously as professional artists, and looking back on this era I am grateful to have been part of this pioneering effort.

The art world in the '70s was a time of great experimentation and investigation in the arts. Artists could still get affordable housing and live in Manhattan, maybe not in comfort, but in community. Jim Monte, a writer and curator at the Whitney, had a theory that cheap rents sustain bold and significant art movements and cited the Paris art movement at the beginning of the century as an example. I think over the past thirty years this theory has proven its truth.

Chapter Nine

Moishe's Delicatessen, a traditional Jewish deli at the corner of Bowery and Grand Street, anchored the artist's community. I was always comforted by its presence as I crossed the Bowery to walk to the subway or to go to the West Village. I remember Moishe's as a plain cement and plate-glass window building. I don't think the grayish Venetian blinds had been opened since it was built. The waitresses were hardboiled New York survivors who had been there since the day it opened, serving up borscht, bagels and lox, pastrami on rye, and cheesecake. You could eat at Moishe's and feel the depth of character of Manhattan. It was part of the history of New York City with funny, tough, unsentimental kindness hidden behind the insults and rudeness of the waitresses. The scuffed red leatherette booths offered an hour of understandable insanity and predictability in the midst of big city chaos.

Moishe's was the lunch spot for local artists like Walter De Maria, Red Grooms, James Rosenquist, Robert Ryman, and others. Walter DeMaria said to me once, "Robert Ryman always has white bread with cream cheese on a white plate at Moishe's." I was amused by this, since Robert was a minimalist painter who worked with white on white. For me, seeing artists around my neighborhood was a reassuring sign of community which I valued. I passed James Rosenquist many times as he headed to Moishe's and finally we said hello to each other, stopping to talk.

Over time my acquaintance with Jim developed into a friendship and eventually we became a couple. During this process, Edward and I separated amicably, having already grown apart. In 1973 I moved alone to Broadway and 19th Street to a small "penthouse" atop an eight-story office building. I had purchased it from Oliver Steindecker, an artist who had been Rothko's assistant up until the time that Rothko died. In fact, it was Oliver who had found Rothko lying dead on the kitchen floor in front of the sink, covered in blood, a razor at his side.

It was often necessary to pay the exiting tenant "key money," usually anywhere from $1,500–$10,000. This supposedly reimbursed the artist for renovations they had

Facing: Autumn Dream, 1973. Acrylic on canvas. 31½" × 30¾".
Top: Manhattan Roofs, 1973. Acrylic on canvas. 30" × 34".

"Well, Well" 1973. Acrylic on canvas. 37½" × 34½". Private collection.

done to the space to make it livable (depending on the skills of the artist...) My key money was $1,500. Oliver was moving to Martha's Vineyard. For some unknown reason he had left behind shoes that he'd purchased from a sidewalk peddler and the odd assortments were in piles all over the floor. My life in the ninth-floor penthouse was actually a shack on the roof in the shadow of a large tower that supplied the building with water, and my front door opened on to the tarred roof of the building. Enclosing the roof was the four-foot parapet of the building, which made a cozy area in which to have a garden in large pots and boxes, chairs, and a table. The bathroom was down a flight of stairs on the eighth floor. I felt safe and homey in this uncomplicated and unadorned environment.

The building had thick floors and I could only occasionally hear hushed voices as office workers walked the stairwells. During the day, the sound of typewriters could be heard through open transoms, and well-dressed office workers came and went. I became friends with the two elevator operators: Stanley, big and overweight, who refused to wear the elevator operator uniform, and Fred, underweight, skin and bones with various twitches, who wore his uniform proudly with knife-pressed creases in shirt and trousers and a spotless cap.

The only offbeat note in the building was the pornography film studio on the third floor. This studio, with no name or address on it, was silent and dark during the day but came alive at night. Since the elevator stopped at 6:00 p.m., I would meet the decidedly *not* office workers as they went to "work" on my long trek upward to the ninth floor.

While the lower Bowery was a pastiche of cultures and people, the area near Gramercy Park where I lived reminded me of my studio in San Francisco. No Golden Gate Bridge, true, but there was Gramercy Park, and I felt that my idiosyncratic housing recreated to some extent the gentle bohemian atmosphere I was familiar with in San Francisco. One of my paintings from this period, *Autumn Dream*, shows the clock on the insurance building on Madison Square, a fixture I saw every night as I went to bed. It reminded me of a friendly moon with moving hands. Its benevolent light was framed by the lofty skyscraper in which it was embedded.

My social and professional lives were unlocked by the renown I gained from the Whitney show and the support I received from Holly Solomon. I enjoyed connect-

Love Letters, 1973. Acrylic on canvas. 30" × 50". New Museum, New York City.

ing with the various artistic talents that made up the creative scene of New York. I was interested in poetry and sat in on readings at St. Mark's Church-in the-Bowery. This venerable landmark was the setting for readings by well-known New York poets. Among them were John Ashbery, Frank O'Hara, Anne Waldman, and Joe Brainard. I felt a common bond between some of these poets and my own art. Later I collaborated on projects with the poet Anne Waldman and did illustrations for a poetry book called *Invention* that Kulchur Press published. Lita Hornick was one of the few poetry patrons in New York City, and she and her husband Morty were instrumental in creating a poetry series at the Museum of Modern Art that featured Allen Ginsberg, Robert Duncan, and other poetry luminaries.

In 1973 I was offered a job teaching art at Sarah Lawrence College and decided to take it. I had been living on the sale of my work up to that point but I liked the idea of a steady income for a while. Three days a week I rode out to Bronxville, a 45-minute train ride from Manhattan, to teach classes. Bronxville, a beautiful New England town, allowed me to see first hand the flaming glory of East Coast autumn.

Jim Rosenquist had been one of my favorite modern painters since I'd first seen his work at the San Francisco Museum of Art's Pop Art show in the 1960s. I loved the painterly quality of his work and his fresh, startling imagery. Unlike the simple icons of many of the other pop art painters, I found complex poetry in the collaging of common elements that he put together. The simple and mundane became lyrical and sensitive, suggesting feelings and metaphors greater than the objects themselves. His painting technique—soft focus, yet strong forms—made solid statements. His work was Pop Art but also a remarkable dialogue with Surrealist undertones. He had imagination.

I spent time with Jim in his studio on the Bowery and had the good fortune to watch him paint. He was a precise craftsman and his painting skills were impeccable. I was continually amazed by his talent and felt humbled in its presence. He mixed paint in giant buckets. Each color had a separate bucket and set of brushes. He had been a billboard painter when he first came to New York City, and he showed me the build-

Jim Rosenquist painting a Times Square billboard.
Photo courtesy of James Rosenquist.

ings in Times Square where he had painted some of the giant towering signs. His job as a billboard painter dangling from scaffolding high above Times Square required him to paint details that would glisten from far across the square. He could paint a bottle to look cold and refreshing or render cigarette smoke evaporating into the atmosphere that could be seen from blocks away. The era of hand-painted billboards is far in the past but they were a rich conveyor of the imagery of daily American life until the mid-twentieth century.

Jim also introduced me to the Sign Painters Guild. At that time, I had toyed with the idea of painting scrims and backdrops for the theater. Jim and I visited a vast backdrop loft in midtown where this magic of drama was created. Forests, cities, and glowing colored panels were sprouting in the middle of great dripping paint cans and yards of gauzy fabric. The loft reminded me of a craftsman guild from the Middle Ages. Although I can't recall why I didn't pursue learning the trade, the image of all that drama remains firmly implanted in my memory.

Jim liked taking me to Horowitz's, the sign painters' brush store in the East Village. I loved buying paintbrushes from Horowitz in his tiny, old-fashioned store. He was, without a doubt, the best brush maker in the city. (Maybe he was the only brush maker in the city.) Each brush was handmade and superior to ordinary artists' brushes in handling and longevity. Billboard painters needed the best. If hairs fell out or brushes lost their shape mid-painting, it would not be easy to get off scaffolding 100 feet in the air to get a replacement. I loaned my favorite brush to a friend, who by accident destroyed it and bought me a replacement. Sadly, to him it was just another paint brush; but the brush he ruined was evidence of Horowitz's craftsmanship and skill. Much later I frequently searched the East Village for his little store and looked for his name in the phone book, but he had died or moved, and taken another era with him.

Jim and I understood each other in a way that I hadn't experienced before in a relationship. The common language of art was a bond between us, an unspoken native tongue. He was able to stretch the bounds of imagination and he was tender and thoughtful with me. Jim was friendly with everyone, loyal to old friends, and informal.

Once, when we were visiting my mother back in Point Reyes, Horace Solomon stopped by for a visit with two collector friends from Paris dressed in pristine Gucci loafers and carefully pressed casual clothes. Rising to the occasion, Jim baked a

Jim Rosenquist working on *Paper Clip*, 1973. Photo by Gianfranco Gorgoni.

strange concoction in my mother's aged stove consisting of grapes, brown sugar, and some other ingredient perhaps best unknown, and served it on a dish towel with holes in it amidst weeds and three-foot-high grass. Point Reyes was still unpretentious and little effort was made to keep up with the Joneses. My mother's house and yard, was, in the words of an English friend, "unruly," and in my opinion, moving towards "decrepit ruin in jungle."

Jim had thin, curling blonde hair ruffled by wind or by his hands and the striking blondeness of Nordic ancestry. He had a sense of style whether wearing clothing he had purchased in the local drugstore or an expensive shop. Robert Rauschenberg once said, "Jim had the face of an angel." I wouldn't go that far, but for me he gave the impression of both fearlessness and poignancy, a combination of traits I found irresistible and seductive.

Even though I had become more comfortable living in New York, I appreciated Jim's casual mastery of the city. He told endless stories about Coenties Slip, an early studio he occupied with Agnes Martin and Kenneth Nolan on the windy tip of lower Manhattan, and various characters and fellow artists that he knew.

When we were living together, collections of nails, paper clips, change, bits of paper, hammers, and screwdrivers would somehow appear anywhere there was a flat space. I found this endearing, and got used to shoving aside odd flotsam and jetsam when sitting down to eat. When he traveled, Jim sent me beautiful postcard collages that were expressive and tender, not exactly written, but more expressive than writing. I would call them visual poems.

I got to know many of his friends and collaborators, including Robert Rauschenberg and Leo Castelli. At the time, Castelli was Jim's art dealer who presided over the most famous and respected contemporary gallery in New York City. The first time I met Leo, Jim and I were in Leo's gallery on West 76th Street attending a small exhibition of Jim's. It was on the top floor of a beautiful and refined four-story town house near Central Park. After entering the gracious wrought-iron door and walking up a winding marble stairwell, we entered a quiet, elegant gallery. At the time Leo had a large Dalmatian dog who padded after him wherever he went. Leo shook my hand, and welcomed us. He was a slender, short, dignified man who personified Italian suaveness. There was a rumor that he had been a secret agent in World War II. Rumor or truth, it was an image that fit his persona. He was a self-contained, immaculately dressed man who radiated mystique. In this first meeting, he took me by the hand into a smaller gallery where there was a long bench covered in pale yellow leather. The Dalmatian followed.

I was a little startled and then apprehensive as Leo bent over the leather bench and pointed at one of the leather-covered buttons that had come undone. He began talking to me about the button unraveling. I didn't know how to respond. Was he flirting with me? Wanting me to mend the button? The Dalmatian's nose was right there between us, pointing to the errant button. Leo's suave demeanor verged on the seductive. His knee grazed mine. Finally I straightened up, gracefully purred (or squawked) that I needed to find Jim and attempted to glide away with a smile. Otherwise I felt I could have been in there forever, coming as unstrung as the button on the buttery leather bench.

I met Robert Rauschenberg in his loft on Lafayette Street. He was a consummate host who enjoyed entertaining. Jim had a lot of affection and respect for Bob, and their meetings were often exuberant. During the evening, as Bob became more sauced and affable, he went to his bedroom closet and pulled out a fur coat.

"For you," he said, handing me a Royal Canadian Mounted Police buffalo coat. Since I didn't have a good winter coat, I loved owning it, knowing there would be few others in Manhattan, or anywhere else in the United States, who'd be snuggled into a buffalo-skin coat on a chilly night.

In 1974 I moved with Jim into a tiny, elderly loft building that was embedded in the midst of the sky-high office buildings of lower Manhattan near Wall Street. Once again a different location in Manhattan offered an entirely different style and ambience.

After five o'clock and on weekends, the entire Wall Street area was a silent forest of steel and glass. It became quite peaceful then, and the sea had a chance to exert its influence as the daytime din expired. The East River was two blocks away and the wind and salty breeze from the New York Harbor dissolved some of the twentieth-century noise and automobile emissions. Old New York seemed to be nearer in time and space, and the feeling of a past life on the waterfront was not far away. After all, giant sailing ships and the madness of port life had existed far longer than the skyscraper upstarts.

Photo of me taken by James Rosenquist, 1973.

My favorite winter food was cooked by an old Russian woman who sold hot dogs and sausages on a corner near our loft. I never saw her face under the several coats she wore to protect herself from the bitter winter river wind, but I do remember her hands, which were inside men's gloves that had the fingers cut out. Like the sausages she served, her fingers were fat and thick. I loved standing in the freezing cold, eating kielbasa dripping with overcooked sauerkraut and oozing mustard out of the bun while hunched Wall Street workers bolted towards their offices. Wall Street, a narrow canyon of concrete, seemed to funnel the winter gales from both the East River and the Hudson.

Chapter Ten

Jim and I also began to spend time in Ybor City near Tampa, Florida, in 1973. Jim had made many prints at the University of South Florida in Tampa and had grown fond of the weather, the area, and had made many friends there. He wanted to spend more time in a warmer winter climate and began exploring the area to find workspaces. He finally rented two empty department stores in Ybor City.

Once a thriving Cuban cigar-making center early in the twentieth century, Ybor City in the '70s was derelict and abandoned. Even so, it maintained a certain charm and dignity. Many of the buildings still had beautiful wrought ironwork and Spanish tiling, and second-story balconies hung over the streets and palm trees caught the breezes from the nearby seaport.

Some vacant blocks still had the occasional grand brick cigar factory standing in the weeds and rubbish. The windows were boarded up and trash blew against the walls, but the majesty of a much older culture still exerted a presence in the ticky-tacky of Florida life. We lived upstairs in one of two old department stores that Jim used as studios on 7th Avenue, the main street of Ybor City. I had a studio across the street in another deserted store. Both spaces had high ceilings and stately columns. I was delighted with the pale pastel buildings, the palms, and the peaceful calm of Tampa. I loved the melancholy beauty of the castoff cityscape of Ybor City and was inspired by the vegetation and color. The streets were mostly empty; a few stalwart enterprises like a drugstore, a barbershop, several restaurants, and tiny Spanish grocery stores still kept their doors open.

My paintings began to reflect some of what I was seeing as I unconsciously absorbed the rich subtropical light and atmosphere. I fell in love with the vegetation, particularly the palm trees. I loved the variety of them, the sounds they made in the rain and wind, and how they caught and reflected light.

I did a series of paintings that was exhibited in the Nancy Hoffman Gallery in 1975 in New York City that expressed some of my feelings about tropical light and space.

Scenes from 7th Avenue, Ybor City, Florida.

Aripeka, Florida.

Our home in Aripeka.

The visual and spatial experience of the area inspired me. Tall vertical buildings that swallowed light no longer surrounded me. I also felt lighter emotionally than I had in New York and frequent trips to Manhattan still kept me in communication with my friends and fellow artists. All it took was a two-hour flight. I didn't know many people in Florida yet but enjoyed the company of Jim and Bill McCain, who helped Jim with construction and studio work. Bill was a bright and knowledgeable man and was an avid reader like me.

As time passed, it became clear that a more permanent residence in the area would be beneficial to us. So we began driving around the Tampa area and exploring the upper Gulf towards Weeki Wachee. We drove north along the coast past New Port Ritchey, a sponge-fishing port (in the early 1970s there were still sponges to be fished), and further. Finally we stopped at Aripeka, a small fishing village on the coast, which could not have had more than one hundred inhabitants. The road wound around through a pristine wooded and jungle area until we drove down a meandering back road overlooking the Gulf of Mexico. When we got out of the car, we were looking at 40 acres of Gulf property that stretched out into the sea. There were palm trees, orchids, bromeliads hanging from the great oak trees and, yes, alligators. An old neglected house peeked out from the jungle. The live oaks were draped in Spanish moss that swung in the wind off the Gulf, which wove in and out of inlets and grassy islands.

The Worker, 1974. Oil on linen. 48" × 65".

Although the sea was shallow along this stretch of coast, dolphins and fish were plentiful. We both fell in love with this isolated tropical land.

One of my favorite painters, Winslow Homer, had painted many wonderful watercolors of the vegetation and water further up the Gulf at Homosassa Springs. He captured the wilderness and untamed jungle that dominated the landscape, and Aripeka still retained much of the same feeling in climate and terrain. Here Jim purchased the 40 acres and built a house and studios. My studio in the house overlooked the tall sea grass and the Gulf of Mexico in the distance. This was the first time since moving to the East Coast that I could see all the way to the horizon. I was in heaven.

I loved the beauty of Aripeka, which in some ways reminded me of West Marin, unpretentious and authentic. I had a fondness for the cultural remnants of Florida Americana from the '30s and '40s, like Weeki Wachee Springs with its underwater mermaids, and down the road, the crumbling ruins of an old dinosaur gas station. The 25-foot-tall dinosaur had originally attracted customers to its pumps but now the peeling gray paint and torn fiberglass only attracted nesting birds. In the back of the gas station was an old building that still sold souvenirs of Florida. This was the Florida of yesteryear and I bought small carved canoes that had "Florida" on the side and ceramic dishes and ashtrays from the 1940s. Much to my dismay, bizarre armadillo bowls from the '40s and real alligator purses were also being sold. As new freeways were built, these odd tourist attractions only attracted the curious, like myself, who took pictures and tiptoed gingerly and respectfully through the detritus of the past.

I was painting and experimenting with collage, with unstretched canvas and with airbrush. I had had a show at the Nancy Hoffman Gallery in 1973 in Manhattan and

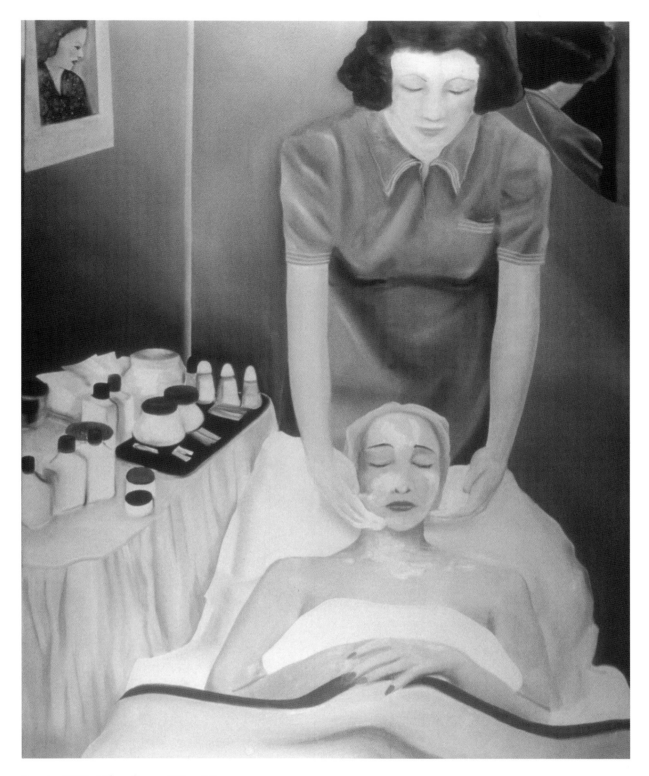

Beauty, 1975. Oil on linen. 71" × 57".

another in 1975. I had shows in Boston and participated in group shows in museums and galleries elsewhere. I felt I was able to still juggle the stretch between New York and Florida.

However, I had altered my entire living situation and emotional structure, and without being consciously aware of it, certain underpinnings of my life had changed. In time I found myself more and more distant from my spiritual practices. The lightness of my spirit became heavier as I didn't make the time to meditate or connect with

Top: The Walk, 1975. Oil on linen. 54" × 71". Private collection. *Above: The Journey*, 1975. Oil on linen. 71" × 57". Private collection.

a community that would support that activity. Although I was social, I also needed a lot of time alone. Like a fish (I am a Pisces), I was refreshed by swimming in the deep and coming to the surface only occasionally. Jim, on the other hand, seemed to thrive with many people around often. I found myself hostessing and preparing food for groups of people, sometimes gallery owners, collectors or European art dealers.

I enjoyed talking and entertaining people but cooking . . . cooking seemed to me to be a dangerous activity using knives and open flames and boiling water. Following recipes was a torture and the disappointment of uncertain results maddening. Once I was determined to make a soufflé that didn't sink to a rubbery pancake, I bought twelve dozen eggs and made soufflé after soufflé, each one worse than the next, trying to figure out what I was doing wrong. Finally I discovered a mistake in the *recipe*. The next soufflé, directions my own, turned out perfectly.

I knew that drinking was a daily ritual for Jim and late afternoon was cocktail hour. I had let drinking go when I was involved with my spiritual practice, finding it a hindrance. Inasmuch as my spiritual moorings had weakened, I was finding the convivial practice of afternoon cocktails attractive. So, after many years without alcohol, I began to drink. At first, it fit in with the social activities of the afternoon and I found it relaxing.

However, I couldn't determine when enough was enough and often drank too much without realizing it. I experienced a lot of the things that troubled drinkers come up against and was either in denial or simply had no understanding of what they meant. I found I was having mood changes that I couldn't control, either very high, or low. I began maintenance drinking with beer and tried not to drink too much or too little. I was not aware that I was self-medicating. What I was really doing was withdrawing from life and ceasing to search for solutions to problems. Since others drank around me, for the life of me I couldn't see why I couldn't. Monkey see, monkey do . . . but the other monkeys were not having the same response as I was and I didn't know it.

I loved Jim, and I loved living in our beautiful home and the adventure of living in the tropics. But I was feeling the stress of navigating so many disparate aspects of my life. I was young and had neither the emotional or psychological tools to guide my life and career into an ongoing rewarding maturity. I felt increasingly uncomfortable. It was not that the alcohol I was imbibing created problems as much as it numbed me to receiving or being open to creative solutions for daily life. Like many people, I had unconsciously created with Jim elements of what I so disliked about my parents' marriage, like the lack of communication and the inequality with which my father treated my mother. As I struggled to keep alive my spirit of artistic adventure, my desire to create a beautiful home, and my artistic life, I found myself for the first time unable to effectively cope on a daily basis. In hindsight, I realized that when I moved from New York, I had brought my inner state along. And in looking back, I am grateful that I was turned inside out, so to speak, and began to see for the first time how powerful emotions and thoughts were.

Meanwhile the New York art world was changing very rapidly. I was still anchored to my creative process but I didn't feel peaceful with it. My work was in a process of trial and error and experimentation that was making me feel vulnerable and left out. I became emotionally chaotic. Even though my investigations into abstract and meta-

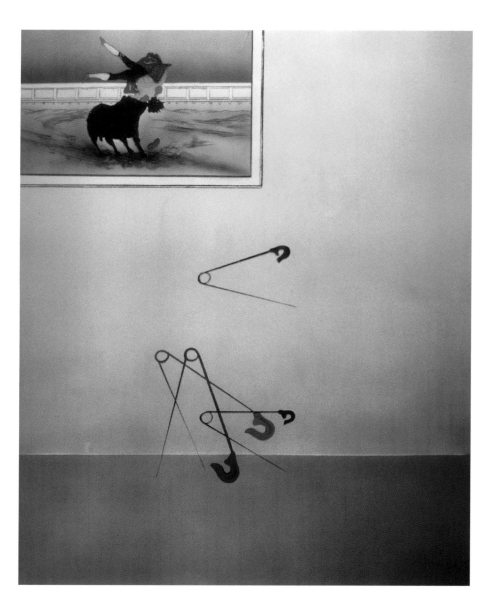

Left: *The Advantage*, 1975.
Mixed media on paper. 44" × 36".
Below: The Alarm, 1975. Mixed
media on paper. 29" × 41".
Collection of Dorsey Waxter.

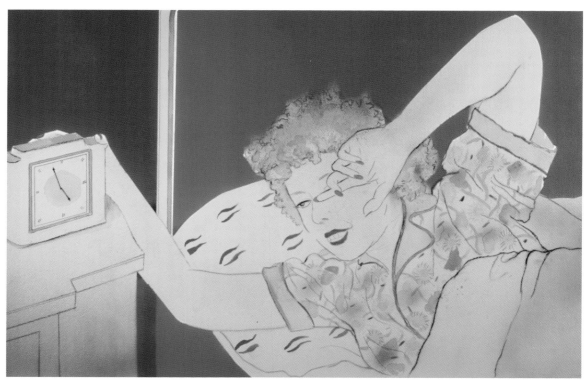

phorical painting were poetic and heartfelt, my sense of well-being was tenuous at best. I didn't understand how much alcohol played a part in this process.

Aripeka was a rugged jungle environment that stretched out into the Gulf of Mexico. It was remote, far removed from the freeways that connected the strings of suburban development outside of Tampa. The environment required a great deal of physical endurance. My strong, feminine side was inundated with the sheer physical demand of living in hot humid temperatures and creating a workable environment. Yes, I could do just about anything, but at what cost to my gentler side? The house was always filled with workers or out-of-town guests who required a great deal of housekeeping. We also traveled back and forth to New York on a regular basis. This lack of continuity added to the feeling that my groundedness was slipping away. I used alcohol to make things okay inside me, and to provide medication against feelings I couldn't manage. Social drinking now became a necessary part of daily management. Regrettably, drinking was my way of coping.

There I was, a housekeeper and hostess, my least favorite roles. Worse, alcohol had taken over to such an extent that by 1978 I realized that I had to leave Jim to get back on track. It was not from a lack of love or feeling for him that I moved back to New York; it was necessary for me to create peace in my inner chaos. My outer world and inner self were falling apart and I needed, or so I thought, to be back in my community of friends. I was unable to communicate this to Jim and lived daily with increasing frustration. I can see now that he may have had many of these same feelings, but we were unable to communicate them to each other as more and more his busy life precluded intimacy. So, after much deliberation and several years of living in Florida, I moved back to New York City in 1978.

He's Gone, 1975. Mixed media on paper. 33″ × 53″.

chapter Eleven

In spite of the grief and despair I felt, I was able to keep my outer life in order. I moved temporarily into a sublet at Westbeth, an artist's co-op in the West Village on the West Side Highway. Since my studio was on a high floor I had a beautiful view of the Hudson and singular sunsets over the New Jersey Palisades. The rotting piers and dilapidated West Side expressway that stretched towards the bottom of Manhattan Island made enticing playgrounds for bicyclists and walkers. The Hudson didn't evoke the images of the nineteenth century that the East River did but being close to water was refreshing and healing. I loved the sky and horizon stretching past New Jersey, and I delighted in roaming through the puzzle of streets that was Greenwich Village.

I began to paint full time and put together a new body of work. I reconnected to the art world and made new friends. I was bereft without Jim and would continue to feel his loss for many years, yet I did feel I was back on course with my own life, despite my continued drinking. My new paintings finally (and, I felt, successfully) incorporated and expressed a certain solid abstraction, emotional depth, and humor.

Patricia Hamilton, the lively owner of the Hamilton Gallery on West 57th Street, saw these works and liked them so much she included me in her roster of artists. In 1978, she asked me to join the Hamilton Gallery. Patricia, with her associate Jay Gorney, put together an interesting mix of mid-career and well-known artists. Louise Bourgeois, Isaac Witkin, John Willenbecher, Deborah Remington, Auste, David Hare, Peter Reginato, and Mia Westerlund Roosen were among the artists who contributed to a superb environment in which to show my work.

I had three exhibitions that were warmly received, that sold well, and were written about favorably. John R. Clarke, an art historian and critic who was teaching at Yale University, wrote a review for *Arts Magazine* that featured a detail of one of my paintings on the cover.

Later, in 1998, John wrote, "Image, Technique and Spirituality in Susan Hall's New Work" for *Arts Magazine*. John wrote another long article about me for the Wom-

Facing: The Card Shark, 1978. Acrylic on stretched Arches paper. 36" × 24".   *75*
Collection of John Willenbecher. *Top:* Ten White Street, my new home.
Photo by David W. Dunlap, *The City Observed*, 1979.

Night Train Express, 1981. Acrylic on canvas. 6' × 12'. Private collection.

an's Art Journal in 2000 entitled "Finding Her Center." Both are in-depth analyses of my painting style and technique. The articles also discuss my philosophy and imagery in a thoughtful and knowledgeable manner. I did several very large paintings that were well received and the art critic William Zimmer wrote a glowing review in the *New York Times* about *Night Train Express,* which was purchased and found a home in the Chase Manhattan building.

I enjoyed the friendship and community of the Hamilton Gallery artists and felt my painting was developing and growing. I used a strange and unexpected mix of metaphor, drawing, and paint to create deeply felt and subconsciously driven paintings. My art became a large expansive vessel for containing the melancholia I felt so keenly. The energetic, creative buoyancy I had previously known melted into a kind of amorphous despondency. The hardest thing for me to do was to keep moving. Curiously, I had very little identity with the positive things happening to me. Outside accomplishments did nothing to mitigate my sadness or to give me self-confidence. On the inside I was experiencing darkness. In time, this inner landscape that seemed so bleak was to be the catalyst for a deepening of my creative spirit. Unaware to me, as the chaos deepened, my heart and feelings did as well, but the fruits of this soul searching were not to be experienced for many years.

In 1979, I pooled funds with a friend of mine, Julie Sylvester, who worked with the Dia Art Foundation, to purchase the top floor co-op of a beautiful cast-iron building on White Street in what is now known as Tribeca. There were other artists living in this grand old building. The first floor was owned by a mechanic who restored old printing presses and resold them in South America. The ancient elevator was accessed through his maze of grimy printing presses and greasy machinery. At one time in the 1870s the building had been a department store and the architectural details on the building were elegant and regal. My loft was about 1,500 square feet with a ceiling that sloped from 15 feet in the studio area to nine feet in the back where I lived. It was a comfortable place to paint large or small works.

Once again, another aspect of the history of New York opened its pages to me, giving my life substance and character. True, my loft didn't have views, just blank white walls at the back and fire escapes. But I kept it Zen-simple with little furniture and a sparse kitchen so that the space was a calm refuge from the outside world. The remainder of the time that I lived in New York was spent in my beloved loft.

Down the center of the loft, slender pine columns rose with dignity. At one point I took all the layers of paint off the columns so that I could enjoy the flawless and knotless tight grain of ancient pine trees. Underneath a hundred years of grime and paint, the dense heart pine could easily have been used for masts on sailing ships in the nineteenth century.

Artists, creative people, and various small businesses occupied the neighborhood. In the tiny triangle between Varick and West Broadway was a nursery that almost gave a park-like feeling to the neighborhood. That is, if you allowed yourself to forget it was surrounded by a ten-foot-high chain link fence. The neighborhood was safe for a single woman and I had many friends in the area. I loved my space to work and paint in, and to entertain friends and people in the art world.

Across the street and nearby lived Elizabeth Murray, David Salle, Louisa Chase, Red Grooms, and many other well-known New York artists. The area was not gentrified yet but the exquisite cast-iron and brick buildings and the wide streets had a sophisticated ambience that SoHo lacked. Magoos, the Mudd Club, the Lower Manhattan Ocean Club, and the Odeon were all popular local hangouts to meet for drinks and socializing.

Alcohol had always been popular in the art world and had become a constant in my life. I drank way too much and had a hard time controlling my usage. When cocaine and drug use became fashionable I thought, "Why not?"

Top: Lightning Strikes Again, 1978. Acrylic on stretched Arches paper. 36" × 24". Private collection. *Below: Portage*, 1978. Acrylic on stretched Arches paper. 36" × 24". Private collection.

Top: The Four Cards, 1979. Acrylic on Arches paper. 30" × 24". Private collection. *Below: Autumn Chemistry*, 1982. Acrylic on canvas. 4' × 6'. Collection of Richard Brown Baker.

Night Flight, 1979. Acrylic on canvas. 6' × 8'. Private collection.

I was able to rationalize drug and alcohol use and deny the effect it had on my life. My emotional intensity increased, as did my feelings of alienation even though I seemingly was active and socially engaged. Work remained my consolation and refuge. Like many addicts I made no connection between my substance abuse and the effects it was having on my life. Ironically, my paintings were welcomed in the art world and most sold. Articles and reviews conveyed to me the feeling that there was an appreciative audience for my work.

However, I was at the same crossroads as after my Whitney show. True, I felt more confident about creating a workable life in New York City and there was less chaos in my life. But, deep down, I felt an existential pull towards greater meaning. Living in

Left: Rachel, 1980. Chalk and charcoal on paper. 39" × 27½". Collection of Jay Gorney. *Right: Deer Isle*, 1980. Chalk and charcoal on paper. 39" × 27½".

Left: Mad Mime, 1980. Conté and charcoal on paper. 35" × 45". *Right: Summer Storm*, 1980. Conté and charcoal on paper. 35" × 45".

Night Light, 1979. Acrylic on canvas. 6' × 12'. Private collection.

New York did not dispel deeper yearnings and nagging feelings. I had no idea what this meant or how to go about discovering what it was that was bothering me. I seemed to have the same paucity of direction that I had in San Francisco years earlier, before I moved to New York City. The unwritten instructions I had received at birth, and which I had unconsciously followed in faith, had now disappeared as I scrambled to make adjustments to the world.

By 1982, my addictions were noticeably taking their toll. I continued rationalizing but found it harder to make up excuses for being late for events or dinner parties. "She can't come, she has the flu again," said unaware friends to explain my absences. I had the "flu" a lot and outrageous hangovers that sometimes lasted days. I no longer had any control over my drinking and drug use. At times I could have one or two drinks and stop. Other times I would drink uncontrollably until I passed out. I could still present a public façade of someone who looked good. When I went out socially, I dressed carefully and made sure that I didn't drink so much that my words would slur and I would have a difficult time walking straight. But the drinking episodes increased and my attempts to stop completely failed.

By September 1982 I hit bottom with alcohol and realized that I had to do something about it. A friend, Judy Hudson, took me to an Alcoholics Anonymous meeting and I began to attend on a regular basis. What had initially appeared to be a disaster—after all, who wants to think that the sum total of their lives has ended in a room full of drunks drinking bad coffee and eating stale cookies—turned into a life preserver. Little did I know joining A.A. would help me make a giant U-turn in my life.

At that time, A.A. was not discussed in polite company and certainly was not held in the high regard it is now. There were no treatment centers, no endless books written about recovery from addiction, no celebrity testimonials from classy rehab centers. Dingy ill-lit church basements and worn-out folding chairs in smoke-filled rooms was the general décor and ambience.

Chapter Twelve

I immediately felt a connection with the people in A.A. The common goal of letting go of alcohol made social interchanges helpful and inspiring. Since the only way to get sober was to be honest, relationships were established without guile. Several aspects of the program fit well for me. There were no fees, and though it was a program of spirituality, the spirituality was defined by one's self. One's higher power was truly one's own. There was no hierarchy or power structure to the organization. There were no rules or regulations besides having a desire to stop drinking. Amazingly, I soon began to reshape my life with this support and connection. Since I no longer put a lot of effort into impressing people (mostly trying to impress them that I wasn't drunk), I could begin to let my cautiousness down and trust people more.

I had forgotten how to access and nurture my inner life. I had intense emotions and strong feelings and desires but had no tools or skills for shaping a life. As I learned how to nurture my inner life by letting go of addictions to drugs and alcohol, a space developed that allowed new things to come in. I began to eat better—or, should I say, I began to eat. Since I could predict where I would be and could trust myself to show up for commitments, I felt more self-control as anxiety began to lessen. I could think more clearly. The chasm that addictions created between my emotional and intellectual responses now began to heal.

The Hamilton Gallery closed during this time and I had more time to evaluate my work. My paintings seemed inadequate and I was dissatisfied with them technically. As I continued to awaken, I wanted more from my art. I wanted to slow down and experience painting in a more contemplative way.

Many of my social connections were not pertinent to what I was going through, and I let most of them go for lack of time and attention. As I opened myself to introspection, I found myself drawn to forms of healing and spirituality: Tibetan and Zen Buddhism, Sufism, healing aspects of Christianity (especially the Episcopalian church in Manhattan), the Quakers, American Indian cultures, Subud, Intensive Journal workshops,

Facing: Two Heads, 1982. Oil and acrylic on canvas. 41¾" × 34". *Top: Country Life*, mixed media on canvas. 42" × 70".

85

and healing techniques and contemplative prayer with Father Keating, the Trappist monk. All of these ways of approaching spirituality were based first in experience, not intellectual concepts about experience. Gradually, I learned that all of my senses could be gateways to reality if I studied my responses carefully enough.

I lived close to the Open Center in Manhattan, which had lectures, workshops, and programs about science, philosophy, and psychology, as well as contemporary and traditional spiritual practices. I attended every class, workshop, and lecture that remotely appealed to me. I felt I had been starving for substance in my life. Perhaps *addiction* to so-called substances was a substitute for the real thing. Gradually I selected ideas, philosophies and practices that felt right to me. Most notable was a renewed trust in the existence of the self. Since I had lost touch with this basic belief because of addictions, I slowly familiarized myself with the physical senses of hearing, seeing, touch, and smell. Babies naturally have preferences and choices but learn though culture that some are okay and others are not. I saw that throughout life from time to time I would have to begin at a place of innocence to reset my compass. I needed to let myself be guided by an inner sense of rightness and intuition, my own North Star, rather than compasses outside myself. I discarded mental constructions that were hierarchical, rigid or arbitrary and began to favor the density and intricacy of ordinary life. Wonder and awe again replaced ideas I had been taught to follow or believe without careful examination.

Invention, 1982. Oil and acrylic on canvas. 42" × 64½".

Shadow Express, 1982. Oil and acrylic on canvas. 45" × 105".

I began to see that life was rich with complexity and interconnected in ways that a casual examination did not always reflect. I discovered the interdependence of life and felt comfort and solace in it. I experienced my world as warm and friendly and I had a sense that I belonged in it. I was able to let go of the notion that I was isolated or estranged. I felt that I was an essential part of the fabric of existence and that I didn't need to prove this fact and belief intellectually.

Chapter Thirteen

Drawing a new breath, I approached my art with simplicity. I began to recover, discover, and uncover a process of art making which had deeper significance to me. Painful and cumbersome as it was, once again I let go of my previous artistic identity to explore a new one. I allowed myself endless time and space for exploration and experimenting.

I didn't rely on my previous ideas and abilities to support what I was doing. Everything was new and untested to me. As frustrating as it was to let go of familiar work habits, I was no longer willing to pay the price of deadening my feelings and anxieties. I rejected self-medication of any kind and began to see how valuable all feelings were to my unfolding process. Body sensations and pain, emotional sensations and feelings all informed me about how I was reacting to my world. My mind became a servant to the totality of my being, not the other way around. As a result, I began to gradually experience a shift in perspective and outlook that eventually completely changed my art.

The emotionally wrenching pain and conflicts of the past years suddenly shifted into a different perspective. As I explored each troubling issue I found that seeming opposites were recombining or evolving into spacious new concepts. For instance, clashes I had about *power* in my life became generous and comfortable when I defined power as *self*-empowerment and not power *over* others. Self-*acceptance* was a more expansive word than self-*improvement*. Self-*acceptance* implied that one belonged on the planet Earth in the first place. Self-*improvement* implied I had to improve myself for someone or something. In the latter case, I was comparing myself to something else and usually finding myself in an inferior position.

I began to learn the importance of faith and humility. These ideas removed me from the center of the universe. I was slowly becoming a part of the world naturally and effortlessly without having to prove myself.

Little by little, I began to reframe basic notions of myself. I came to see I was a stew-

Little by little, I began to reframe basic notions
of myself. I came to see I was a steward for
my gifts and abilities—physical, artistic, and
intellectual. This meant I had to nurture
my talents like a gardener and share them
with the world. I slowly began to change
my attitude about my purpose. I finally
acknowledged that the art scene did not
offer me much in the way of inspiration
and nurturing. To continue the garden-
ing metaphor, the New York soil I was living in lacked
enough nutrients for me to fulfill my aspirations. I didn't fit in
any longer, and if I was really honest, I didn't want to.

Having realized that, where to start? What were
the steps to becoming this new artist and creator?
It seemed reasonable and honest to begin with what
I already was doing in my work. I slowly and carefully began to observe how I painted, to observe what
felt real and vital to me and what did not. I wrote these
observations down in notebooks. If I felt an intensity and vitality that
seemed to come from a spark of some sort, I used this
observation to point my way. I developed a habit of
sitting a few minutes after I painted to jot down
feelings, reflections, and anxieties. By giving this
internal voice space, I also gave myself credibility and
self-respect.

I became like a child in front of a table filled with all of the foods in the world
who has the opportunity to pick whatever she likes. In time, I believed, the child would

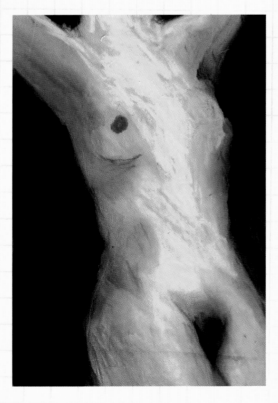

Torso I. Pastel on paper. 24" × 36".

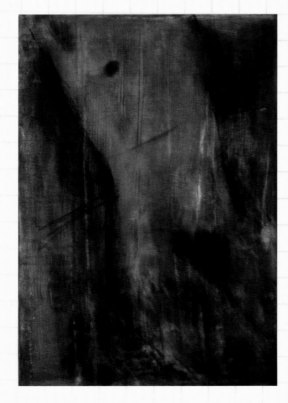

Torso II. Pastel and oil on canvas. 24" × 36".

pick what was best for her growth. Without direction or supervision, I could pick whatever appealed to me in my work. I knew this assumption left out many things, but for a start I used my child self to make choices. If the choices weren't beneficial, I could try another method. I noticed that much of what I was taught about art making was the result of what my teachers had been taught themselves and didn't come from direct experience. For me to have an authentic and valid artistic experience, I wanted to find what worked for me, what made me feel alive and passionate.

For example: while drawing a model with charcoal I might make a drawing that was in correct proportions with properly shaded muscles and anatomy. I would feel that the drawing succeeded in replicating what was in front of me and I would feel a sense of accomplishment from this effort. Then I would draw the model again; this time paying attention to my internal responses while I worked. The finished drawing might be accurate or not. But the feeling inside me was alive and heartfelt.

I realized how important the sense of touch was and how it was a bridge between the inner realm of the self and the outer world. I had learned to paint in school by using a brush. A brush extends the hand and lengthened the distance between the hand and the painting. What would happen if I were to eliminate this distance from the paint to me? I reasoned that I would be that much closer to the source of my own painting inspiration. The fingers, with their multitudes of nerve endings and sensitivity, would not be distanced from the painting by an added length of brush. I began painting with my fingers and hands directly on the paper and canvas. This felt very alive. Whatever I was feeling inside was then directed instantly to the paper and canvas.

However, I noticed that I was still looking; either observing my paintings as I painted or directing the imagery from the start. I wondered what would happen if I couldn't see what I was doing? What would happen if my connection to what I was doing was based on touch and not channeled through sight? I experimented by turning

the lights off and painting in the dark. I noticed a more direct connection between hand and self that allowed me to express and observe my feelings, my heart and my mind. There was a smaller gap between inner and outer which created an immediacy and spontaneity in the painting experience.

I liked painting blind, but I wanted a way to stay on the canvas, so I experimented

by painting with sunglasses on, sometimes two or even three pairs to cut down light without destroying a sense of the surface I was working with. With three sunglasses on I kept the electricity and vitality of my original creative impulses and could also sense the general boundaries of what I was working on. I realized that I had been taught to rely primarily on my vision to develop composition and color. I dimmed the lights in the room and put on several pairs of sunglasses until I could just barely see the area I was working on. (I was alone and happy no one could see how I had turned into an eerie giant insect!) I could still tell the colors apart even with several pairs of sunglasses, but I could not make out specific details.

When I had been taught how to paint, mind and eyesight were emphasized. By cutting down the visual connection in my experiments, I let go of that kind of control. Letting go of the intellect and eyesight allowed me to pay attention to what was going on inside of me, namely feelings. It was not just emotions I wanted to explore but the symphony of body sensations, breathing, thoughts and sounds that drifted by my consciousness. I wanted to be alive to my responses to the environment: noises, smells, even the felt sense of the room I was in. Without consciously realizing what I was doing, I was putting myself in the on-flowing present, the *now* of reality. This process, repeated enough, became a practice for me. I was in the river of life with my art. Not moving parallel with it or conflicting with it, but swimming along in it.

I found that by gently focusing my attention on different parts of my body while I was painting, I could increase the energy flowing there. Then, I found that if I touched my stomach while I was painting, the intensity of connection between hand and stomach intensified and was energized. If I touched my head while I was working, that connection became the guiding force for the energy coming from my hand and onto the paper. I couldn't *control* these influences and sensations, but by becoming aware of them, I could allow them to have their own voice. For instance, one day when I was painting, I noticed I had a painful headache. I tried an experiment; I closed my eyes, put one hand on my head, and allowed the sensations of pain to enter my focus and attention. Continuing with my eyes closed, I inwardly visualized a channel for the pain to move onto the piece of paper. I dipped my brush in the black ink I'd chosen. I slowly allowed the brush to move as I experienced the pain. Without intellectualizing, interrogating or quizzing myself I could make new connections with my creative process.

I had come upon a crucial and important point: I had to trust without questioning that this process worked without any intervention from critical thinking. By this I mean whether or not I had skepticism about the process if I gently continued and allowed the pain in my head to express

Bridge and Train, 1985. Oil on canvas. 24" × 18".

itself through the brush on paper I would get results. I tried this experiment many times with different parts of my body. Results could be the cessation of pain, increased sensations, or a change in the movement of brush or hand. It seemed important to place a hand on the area I wanted to give a voice to. I believe the identification of the body part allowed it to be singled out. Perhaps it was a little like putting your hand on someone who has been crying. Touch gave comfort and also respect to that body part. Every time I did this experiment my experience and the paintings were different. I allowed them to be what they were and did not evaluate them or attempt to change them in any way.

Chapter Fourteen

T his new way of approaching art was accentuated for me by an experience I had during a trip to the Painted Desert, 160 miles of buttes and badlands in Arizona. Every hue of pink, orange, and purple stretches through the rocks and soil. Giant boulders and endless rock formations stir the imagination towards the sublime or the ludicrous. I stopped the car on a seemingly empty road to stretch my legs and noticed a small path through some boulders on the side of the road. Curious, I walked down between the rocks. Within a minute or two, I lost sight of the car and the road. The huge boulders surrounding me muffled all sound. Above me, one lone hawk arched into the sky. I stopped and took a couple of deep breaths to slow down. I wasn't prepared to be catapulted into such a different reality so quickly. As I quieted down from the jolt, I was taken aback to see marks on the rocks. These marks, I soon realized, were pictographs that covered the huge boulders. Some were abstract and some were simple drawings of birds, animals, and people. These pictographs were the artwork of humans who had lived here long before, maybe hundreds of years, maybe thousands.

Like a radio switching from AM to FM I found myself on a different wavelength. My intuition was telling me that this art had been painted not from the eyes, but from another part of the body. It was as if the heart, not the head, had eyes. It was as if aliveness in all parts of the body of the artist had been voiced instead of an intellectual concept. What might be interpreted as a primitive portrayal of an image was not that at all. It was a much more visceral connection between the artist and the image. The impact of this awareness was powerful and I knew I could spend years exploring this idea.

I used this incident to substantiate the insights I had been having in my painting experiments. My creativity was becoming much more alive by using more senses than eyesight alone. This revelation was startling. I realized I had been hindered by my limiting education, which dealt with *picture* making and using the eyes as the primary tool for constructing images.

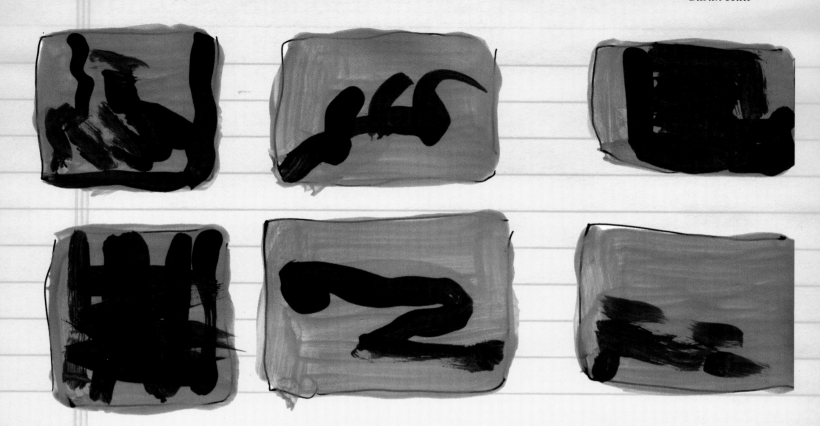

The significance of the pictographs in the desert was not accessible through my previous art knowledge. This was a different visual paradigm; one that was powerful and direct. I didn't fully comprehend what I was experiencing, but I knew I had made a valuable discovery. Back in New York, the experience in the desert inspired me to make further investigations. I discussed my revelations about eyesight and vision with some of my advanced students at the School of Visual Arts who were also interested in the creative process. They, too, were excited. Their experiences confirmed that the visual element of seeing was secondary to something less definable but more comprehensive. Words like self-observing and self-accepting were more vital to creativity than words like criticism and analysis.

This process was not about art therapy, which used interpretation as a tool for getting at suppressed or repressed feelings or experiences. This was a way to attain faith and trust in oneself as a creative artist.

In my studio I expanded my own experimentation. I continued to paint while wearing sunglasses; seeing only the vague outlines of my work area I used black washes. I used this series of simple paintings to observe my feelings and impulses. I made a series of boxes on large sheets of heavy paper, like a children's comic book. In this format painting impulses could continue from box to box. *Movement, not evaluation*, I told myself. Whenever I felt stuck, I moved on to the next box. My ongoing critical analysis of the painting process disappeared, and I noticed an intensity of energy and feeling both within me and on the canvas.

Through experimenting on my own I found the self that is

deeply embedded in consciousness below the surface of daily life. I used myself and my feelings as feedback to determine which experiences worked or didn't. I made notes and drew diagrams, which could be communicated to other people. I felt I was softening the barriers and restrictions to getting beyond ordinary reality. There was great vigor and vitality in what I was finding.

Experimenting, I used paper towels or rags to move the paint around instead of brushes. I painted with two simple colors so I wouldn't be distracted.

In order to make the process even more dynamic I filled the largest sheets of paper I had with boxes in rows. Again, I painted all of the boxes a solid color in regular room light. This time I mixed a larger quantity of black so I wouldn't have to stop in the middle of what I was doing to mix more paint. I had a medium-sized brush, which I kept close at hand.

My preparations done, I was ready to paint when I had darkened the room and put on my funny sunglasses.

(A sense of humor is a must.)

I set a timer for ten minutes. I chose ten minutes since I felt it was a time frame that wouldn't tax my patience and stamina.

I stuck with simple rules for guidelines:

Do not stop once you start painting.

Movement, not evaluation is the goal. If I felt stuck, I simply moved on to the next box. When the timer rang I would stop, put my brush down and turn on the lights.

The energy and emotional impact of these exercises was dramatic. I had kept in mind the rule: *movement, not evaluation* and *whenever I felt stuck, I moved on to the next box*. With the lights turned back up, these works had more life in them than did my thought-out work. My responses vibrated in the same way as they had when I had seen the pictographs in the Painted Desert.

Why was this happening?

Let's look at the first rule: *"Do not stop once you start painting."*

The usual tendency is to paint for a period of time and then stop and look at what you are doing. Then begin to paint again. The observations about the painting made when stopping affect the next step of the painting.

If you *do not stop once you start painting* there is no time for the constraints of evaluation, self-criticism, or second-guessing. No longer is the artist copying the teacher's values or relying on outside information for direction. Instead the artist confronts the artist's experience in the now, allowing a sense of joy to emerge.

For some students, and myself as well, it involved leaving training wheels behind. Anxiety pursued most: "Am I failing?", "Am I fooling myself?", "I will never be famous, well liked, or original doing this," "I will never paint anything again."

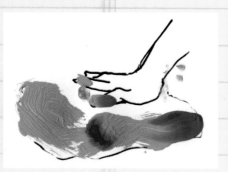

I have heard just about every negative comment a person could make. I too experienced gloomy, defeatist, and fatalistic dreads. But I stubbornly kept on with my own rule: *Movement, not evaluation*. Whenever I felt stuck,

I took a deep breath and moved on. Eventually these admonitions from my
"inner critic" prompted me to give a series of workshops in my studio called
"Getting to know your NO."

These processes gave strength and encouragement to continue despite
negative thoughts or feelings. When students came up against expectations—
cultural, parental, or self-imposed—they now had tools for dealing with them
that were credible and useful. When they had set expectations: "I have to be
perfect" or "My art must sell in order to be worthy," the grip of these expectations
didn't overwhelm their enjoyment of making art.

In all but a few cases, students doing these simple practices found that creativity
and the art-making process were not primarily connected to their eyesight or intellectual concepts. Making art that was driven by outside demands or inner-imposed stric-
tures was not going to make them better artists. And in fact, they would face a time
when making art according to these rules would become increasingly difficult and
even impossible.

Some called it the "creative spirit" or "creativity," or they enjoyed it but didn't feel
they had to name it at all. I used phrases like "the great mystery" or "the ongoing,
on-flowing river of life within." Since I was in academia, where words and concepts
are so important, I was tempted to name this process something that seemed part of the
pedagogical, highbrow world of New York. My qualms about adding emotional and
mental burdens that weighed students down kept me from giving the process an elabo-
rate name.

As a teacher, I began to feel my role was to pass on useful tools to help follow an artistic life. I continued my experiments in the classroom and in my studio. I realized that my rule of *movement not evaluation* was the key to staying in the present. I filled the page with boxes and when I felt stuck on one box, I simply went on to the next, setting a timer for ten minutes or less to create a time frame in which to work. I would paint, then stop when the timer went off then begin a new exercise. Doing this minimized fatigue.

I proceeded, using no more than four colors, continuing to let go of eyesight as the director of my painting. I likened the painting process to the way athletes play tennis. When one is playing tennis, the mind takes a back seat. If the mind is boss, it can't keep up with the faster than lightening signals that are necessary to hit the ball.

The painting process has a tendency to go astray when you stop in the middle to stand back and observe. It's like stopping in the middle of a tennis game and thinking about the ball and where it's going. While you are thinking, you have already missed the ball. Similarly, writers often write their way into what they're really feeling, to get below the layers of awareness. It is easier to write, write, write, and save the editing process for later. With artists, however, I think there is a tendency to stand back and evaluate the ongoing process of painting or drawing. This leads to frustration and anxiety.

I felt the most alive and integrated when I had this primary energy of excitement and inspiration to guide me. *Do not stop once you start to paint.* If you feel stuck, move on to the next box. *Movement, not evaluation* is the goal. Sometimes, no matter what I did, analytic thinking took over or I lost my attention because of fatigue. At that point I would either stop or go on to the next box or another painting. I saved my evaluation for the very end of the process.

Then I put everything aside for a few days before looking at it again. At this time I limited my appraisal to acknowledging what felt the strongest and most alive in my work. I also made a point of spending my time observing and being with the work without making negative comments. I emphasized the positive.

I became aware of the danger of negativity and its debilitating effect on me. If I paused too long or was unaware, I could easily slip into negative internal comments. Some people seem to extend this automatic criticism to absurd ends. Negative comments or put downs of art are not innocent or benign. They can destroy the act of creativity altogether. This is like trying to drive a car with a foot on the brake and the handbrake set. I had received so much criticism about my work during art school that I am surprised I was able to continue being an artist.

A lot has been written about the Inner Critic, and I spent a long time looking at the ways negativity ruled my art. It's a curious human trait to believe that negativity and criticism have more weight and validity than praise and encouragement. I found this to be particularly true in advanced art classes.

Teachers bring their own backgrounds and the way *they* were taught to their teaching of art. Without insight into what motivates them to teach, they are automatically transferring outdated methods, pessimism, and hopelessness to their students. Like bad parenting, a bad teacher can

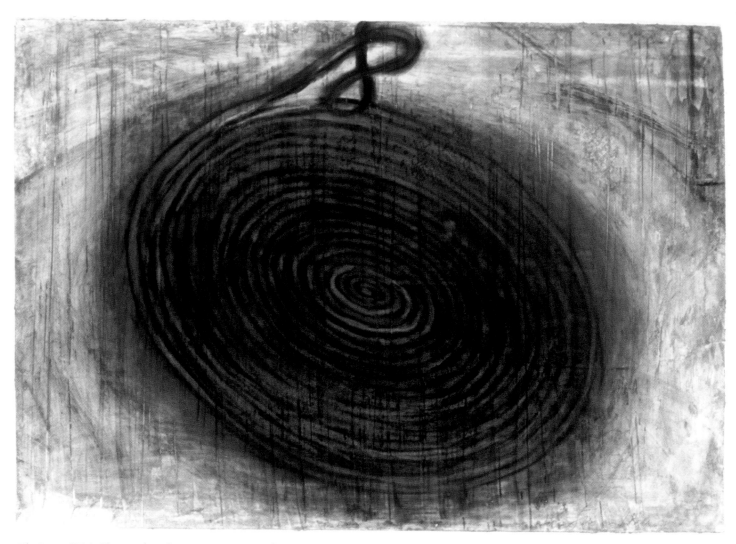

The Rope, 1986. Charcoal and conté on paper. 24" × 36".

be quite self-righteous. As a teacher, I wanted to adhere to the Hippocratic Oath that doctors take: Do no harm.

I didn't feel I had the ethical or moral right to issue judgments and call it a teaching method. Gentle guidance while allowing someone's spirit to emerge: this is the aim of being a teacher, or should be. The student would do the rest themselves out of passion and curiosity. The creative energy of the universe was more than anything I could imagine and I wanted each of my students to feel the greatness of the creative life force for themselves.

I painted several paintings at once. I was a complicated person and artist and I needed a lot of space to express everything I was feeling about a particular subject. I trusted that when I had expressed everything necessary, I could recognize the elements that had enough substance to become a finished piece. I found my sense of self to be expanded far beyond a mental construct. My sense of self as an artist became a means to experience an emotional and total life response that was sweeping and immense.

Chapter Fifteen

By 1989, living in New York City had become intolerable for me. I was beginning to suffer claustrophobia living in a vertical world, and I didn't like shutting down my senses in order to cope with the intensity of the city. The stress and strain of conducting everyday life seemed to be an overwhelming amount of work. As a friend put it, "New York City is where grocery shopping is a contact sport." I spent that summer in Point Reyes for my yearly dose of West Marin nature and returned to the city in the fall to continue teaching at the School of Visual Arts. I still found some pleasure in being with friends, seeing art exhibits and walking in the city, but I didn't feel this was enough to sustain a life. I felt the art community I had formed many years ago wasn't working any longer and I didn't identify with most of the art that I was seeing. Yet I was stubbornly loyal to New York and had bought the absurdity that New York was the axis of the art world. Despite my best attempts to do otherwise, part of me still clung to beliefs that had been true in my life fifteen years before, but were no longer viable.

I was clueless as to how I could create a change in my life that wouldn't be totally traumatic and self-destructive. I wanted to fashion a cohesive, integrated life. I still felt that my many interests, longings, feelings, beliefs, talents, and past history—all the parts of me—were like pinballs rattling against one another. I knew all the parts, but did all the parts know and accept each other? How could I reach a level of self-love and self-acceptance that would create a peaceful, unified person who could be effective? Self-acceptance and self-love seemed to be clichés lacking substance. Yet I couldn't come up with a diving apparatus that would take me below the superficial into the depths of self-knowledge.

Intuition told me to trust that life itself would bring the change that I needed. Once again, I believed on a subconscious level that the unknown, yet knowing, life force would come up with a plan. The great mystery, undisclosed to me and outside my personal abilities to manipulate or control, somehow would evolve into a positive outcome.

Facing: Woman with Shadow, 1987–88. Oil on canvas. 44" × 32".

Top: Canoeing, 1990. Oil on canvas. 24" × 36".

Woman by the Pool, 1986–87. Gouache and charcoal on paper. 30" × 22".

I have always been fond of suspense novels and murder mysteries and read them zealously. I am curious how plots unfold and how the characters and situations interrelate and resolve themselves. My spiritual life is also like that. I am curious and fascinated by life, by its immensity, how it unfolds. I follow clues that are often red herrings or on occasion substantiate my instincts. I am the detective fumbling alone in the dark, tripping over her own feet. Other times, I am the sophisticated sleuth inferring outcomes with nothing more than a bent twig or blade of grass to point the way. Furthermore, every time I choose to specifically name my spiritual beliefs they melt into something else entirely. Then I feel an "Aha!" when I finally know that a broader perspective has appeared. Coming when least expected, it makes even more sense than what I knew before.

The unknown and unknowing, the unnamable, following a path that has clues, inferences, signs, directions, and presence, best describes what my life journey has been about. Hinduism, which has thousands of gods and entities, makes sense. I asked a Hindu friend about her religious beliefs and she replied that Hinduism is very practical. For instance, we need to have a God with hundreds of arms to help us. Why would anyone have a God with only two arms?

At this juncture of my life, without a guide or map, it seemed best to nurture these optimistic beliefs and clues and see what happened.

In my creative process I was grappling with a persistent urge to paint these same vague feelings. My paintings in the late 1980s were large, approximately four and a half by six feet, of single standing women in dark and empty rooms. The form of the figure was revealed by a single edge of light coming from a light source out of the picture frame. In this way, the figures were given form and substance.

I had periodically worked with a model since I was a student and found the female form challenging. I also felt there was an expressive poetry about women that I didn't feel about the male form. In any case I was much more inclined to soften anatomy, and I drew and painted women better than men. I was not disposed to making portraits of specific individuals, although the individuality of specific models was recognizable at times. I pared down all elements in these stark compositions to a suggestion of interior

Two Sailboats, 1989. Oil on canvas. 32" × 45".

Woman on Float, 1989. Oil on canvas. 32" × 45".

Georges Seurat. *The Lighthouse at Honfleur*, 1886. Conté crayon heightened with gouache on laid paper, 24.1 × 30.8 cm. Image copyright © The Metropolitan Museum of Art / Art Resource, NY.

space and the defining ray of light on the form. Often they were framed in turquoise, pale pink or yellow.

Fellow artists found the paintings interesting but the only enthusiasm for show-ing them came from Trabia MacAfee, a newly opened gallery on Greene Street. The director gave me two shows, one in 1989 and the next in 1990. She sold many paintings and was enthusi-astic about my work. The paintings in the 1990 show had the same spareness of composition and form as my work from the previous year, but washes of color and spots of hue gave the dark spaces warmth and life.

I had always loved Seurat's diminutive charcoal and Conté drawings, which were such a contrast to the large pointillist paintings for which he was well known. Less than ten inches in size, Suerat's miniatures commanded a monu-mental scale completely out of proportion to their smallness.

In these humble drawings, Seurat was able

Georges Seurat. *The Veil*, ca. 1883. Conté crayon.
31.5 × 24.2 cm. Réunion des Musées Nationaux /
Art Resource, NY.

to create form that had weight, density, and mass, without heaviness. The charcoal lines were not smeared but drawn with an even pressure of hand and overlapped where density was important. The technique, uncomplicated and plain, had an unadorned frankness. For me, there was lightness in his images; light as in physical weight and light as in transmitting luminescence.

I was not interested in imitating these master-pieces, but I wanted to understand how Seurat had graphically attained a complex impact in such an unpretentious manner. I was more inspired by them than most paintings and draw-ings I had seen. They captured the density of three-dimensional form and the joy of seeing it on a two-dimensional surface.

I was refreshed by the spareness of Seurat's technique. The images were *enough* just the way they were. I wanted my art to be grounded and spacious like them, to live from the inside out, to have weight, substance and density without being overworked or pretentious.

Thinking about it now, this was also the way I wanted to be as a person. I wanted to be straightforward and strong in myself. Seurat's charcoal drawings provided me with plenty of guidance for frankness and sincerity.

Georges Seurat. *The Orange Merchant*, 1886. 31 × 24 cm. Réunion des Musées Nationaux / Art Resource, NY.

The sum total of a person—emotions, spirit, and physical structure—added up to meaning and substance. Without consciously being aware of it, I was striving to achieve an art that reflected this corporeality and density. Spiritual and emotional essence were as important as physical essence: mass, weight, shape, and structure. These ideas resonated with me and I felt a parallel in my quest to become an artist and a person.

This is what I sought, most of the time unconsciously. This was a primary driving force, like birds migrating, or salmon swimming upstream to fulfill their destiny.

It has become increasingly clear that answering and being true to myself is more important to me than reacting to the outside world. As an artist, the satisfaction and fulfillment I feel in honoring my heart's desire is more meaningful and exciting than shaping my life towards career achievement. I increasingly see myself as having certain gifts and abilities that I want to share with the world. I have let go of the notion that I have to fit into the world and instead I focus on being the best me I can possibly be. Perhaps most artists have very different goals and find this intimate personal connec-tion with their work intolerable, but for me, the goal of personal growth and reflecting it in my artwork is a vital aspect of my artistic vision. I can see now that as I became more internally steady, my artistic compositions also became more stable and grounded.

Left: Stone's Cottage. 1989. Oil on canvas. 44" × 32". Private collection. *Right: Woman in Pool.* 1989. Oil on canvas. 44" × 32". Private collection.

Seurat's little drawings were ultimately more symbolic, their metaphor more impor-tant to me than their technique. My paintings of single women emerging from the dark with thin slices of light to give them form were manifestations of myself emerging to occupy my mortal tangibility. Looking back at this period, I can see I really was begin-ning to paint from the inside out.

At this point, I asked myself, what would it mean to reverse this idea and paint from the outside in? For many years I did just that and I felt this quest was not satisfying. It would be like learning Seurat's charcoal drawing technique and thinking *that* alone would make me as good as Seurat. There are all kinds of variations of this type of put-ting the cart before the horse. It is making the intellect the driver. It is more comfort-able to delude oneself into thinking that the artistic process has some tangible intellec-tual pathway that can be spoken about with reasonable clarity.

Painting from the inside out, on the other hand, is an exploration of mysticism, a spiritually contemplative journey. An odyssey of not understanding, but blind trust, like the ideas from the "Cloud of Unknowing," an anonymous spiritual treatise from the fourteenth century.

Facing: Lisa by the Pool, 1989. Oil on canvas.

Chapter Sixteen

By the late 1980s the number of people engaged in the art world had exploded significantly. I felt a loss of community and warmth. A factor in my own work and, I see now, in my life, was the need for intimacy. In New York, making *original* art had become more important than making *meaningful* art. I realized that being an artist was a way of life and its own reward. If this was a romantic ideal, I could easily live with it because it encompassed aspirations and goals beyond myself that were not easily accessible or attainable.

In the end, I had to deal with who I really was and not who I wanted to be in life. I was drawn to spiritual and contemplative elements. Feelings of awe, wonderment, and reverence took precedence over intellectual or career accomplishments. These feelings were what truly motivated my artistic endeavors.

To my surprise, my fears, in the end, were alleviated by the deep and profound changes and evolution taking place in the world. As the pervasive use of computers and the Internet increased, connections with people all over the world became easy. This enabled my work to be accessible to New York or the Siberian steppes, with equal ease. Also, the increasing evidence of the denigration of the planet placed a focus on West Marin, my birthplace, as a functioning wildlife area still in fairly pristine condition close to the dense urban population of the San Francisco Bay Area. The people of West Marin are pioneers in preserving ranch and farmland and enforcing strict regulations regarding development. West Marin has about two million visitors a year who come to the area to participate not only in its beauty, but to exchange dialogue with environmentalists and to develop political and philosophical ideas beneficial to the planet. As I write this, Point Reyes has become a magnet for poets, writers, artists, and innovative thinkers.

I decided to make the move back to West Marin. I moved in with Steve McKinney, with whom I had developed a relationship during my annual summer visits. He was living with his two beautiful daughters, Lia and Kacy, in a house in Inverness

Above: 10 White Street, New York City. *Photo by John Willenbecher.*
Below: 50 Lorraine Avenue, Point Reyes Station.

Park, three miles from Point Reyes Station and a mile from White House Pool. I asked a realtor friend of mine to put my loft in Tribeca up for sale. Gone were the grease, grime, and ancient elevator. Tribeca had become a very fashionable place to live, not just for artists but also for professionals and the upwardly mobile. In 1992, I received news that a tenant in my building wished to purchase my space. I flew back in the autumn and quickly sorted through twenty years of living in New York City. After throwing out more than I thought I could possibly throw out, soon I was hiring a moving company to move the remainder of my possessions and artwork to my mother's home in Point Reyes Station.

Arriving in Point Reyes, the moving van driver shook his head in dismay that I had left a coveted Tribeca address for this humble, lower-middle class postwar neighborhood, complete with dogs sleeping in the middle of the street. My Point Reyes studio was only 400 square feet; my New York belongings looked completely out of place. The driver truly felt sorry that my status in life had been downgraded to this shameful level. Sadly he shook his head, "Living in the sticks—will you like it?"

His outspoken remark was further strengthened when he was greeted by my wobbly 80-year-old mother and Steve, whose wild and wiry hair and secondhand clothing must have confirmed my status as a loser of New York cool.

The Path, 1995. Oil on canvas. 11" × 16".

Chapter Seventeen

I t seemed it would take a great deal of time to establish a new identity and presence in West Marin. I was turning 50 and finding myself in a new family with Steve, Lia, and Kacy. Lia, the oldest daughter, was studious and serious. She was singularly beautiful with long, tightly-curled hair like her father. Kacy was tall and slim like Steve. With their dark eyes and masses of rich dark curly hair, Steve and his daughters could have been mistaken for Spaniards. With my straight blonde hair, I sometimes felt like a black and white photo next to their exotic looks. Later, Steve's hair began to thin, Lia trimmed her profusions of curls, and Kacy, the youngest, cut her hair off completely and went for the bald look. All three radiated a special quality, a hint of depth and richness of spirit that was not confined to their physical beings or beauty. I felt I could write poetry in their presence.

As Lia grew, she became involved with cooking, baking, organic gardening, and plants. At one point she ran Deborah's Bakery in nearby Inverness Park, making incredible breads and pastries that people would line up to buy. Kacy, always adventurous, high-spirited, and public minded, became a political geographer studying the ramifications of genetically modified organisms in India and Brazil. It would be easy to stop with this serene family picture, but, in truth, getting to know gifted teenage girls with developing and individuating personalities was a real challenge. I sometimes felt that I had gotten on the wrong subway and ended up lost in the Bronx, with only instinct to guide me. In time, nature took its course, and we all learned to trust and accept one another.

As my mother aged, I could not bear the thought of her moving from where she'd lived since the '40s. She didn't drive; her entire life was her yard, neighbors, and the village life of Point Reyes Station. She was involved with my sister and her children who lived in Belmont, south of San Francisco, but I couldn't picture her living there. Moving back to Point Reyes satisfied the commitment I made to ensure that she could continue to live in her home until she died. Living in Inverness Park with Steve meant

Facing: Homeward Bound, 2005. Oil on linen. 11" × 16". Collection of Celeste and Robert Ward. *Top:* Our cabin in Inverness.

115

My mother, Avis Hall, in her garden.

I was close enough to attend to her needs and still have privacy for myself. Years earlier, I had turned the garage on her property into a summer studio space; now it was my full-time studio.

I loved my mother for her friendliness and kindness, for her immense, wild, tangled garden with its hubcap birdbaths, flowers, and huge blackberry patch. Her berries were used every year in the jam offered by the seniors at the yearly Crafts Fair in Point Reyes, a much-coveted delicacy that quickly sold. On the other hand, our verbal communications were not deep or informative. She still locked her emotions inside of herself except for pleasantries. She was hard of hearing, and I found out when she was 80 years old that she had no hearing at all in one ear, the result of a childhood accident. No wonder I never felt heard by her! I recalled the many times throughout my youth frustratingly trying to get her attention and receiving a blank stare or being ignored. So this was the secret to so much of our lack of communication! Caring for her required constant patience, which I had little of, and forbearance, even less. As my mother aged, I was able to add a sense of humor, which I developed in some measure. Kacy, now a full-blown teen with dyed orange hair and tattoos, ended up being the only person my mother liked to have around her.

The garage studio I was using required all kinds of adjustments to work in. Steve, with his imaginative carpentering skills, kept the hand-built look of the garage, yet added touches that made it viable as a studio. It had been created by my mother and father from scraps of lumber during World War II when wood was scarce, and was cobbled together with lumber found on the beach and odd pieces reclaimed from previous projects. I simplified my artistic needs to a table and paints, and allowed myself to sink back to those other times in my life when I had been constricted to unassuming spaces. I created in this new studio a meditative space where I allowed all of the tools and capabilities I had taught myself in other times of my life to guide my painting process. I slowly began painting and drawing, unconcerned with the results, simply allowing my artistic life to unfold much the same way as I had long ago in North Beach.

I also made time in the next months to reacquaint myself with hiking trails I had known from my youth, wandering on the beach, and taking in this new, old life. I bought a used VW convertible and delighted in the luxury of being in the total sensual surround of West Marin. Nothing pleased me more than taking old roads I had not been on for thirty years and seeing with adult eyes what I had been so reverential of as a youth. The tumultuousness and sorrow of life, things done, things undone, things not done but wished for, were given a chance to be aired, to be felt in their entirety, either to dissipate or to be resolved.

Steve and I lived only a mile or so from White House Pool, the bend in the road where I had enjoyed my first memories of playing by the stream in the woods. The old

Acapella. 2005. Oil on linen. 11" × 16".

white farmhouse had been torn down in the 1960s, but the current owners kept the orchard trees and the creek preserved in its original wild beauty. I loved living with Steve in our cottage in the woods in the middle of the smells of bay leaves and pines and the multi-storied shadows and glimmers of light. Every morning I was delighted to greet this world full of birds singing and the occasional clatter of deer hooves as they veered away from my presence.

I felt a loss of a part of myself by leaving what many considered the center of the art world. Certainly, I missed the woven fabric of contacts I had built up for so long, and perhaps I even missed the constant struggle of surviving in New York, which for me felt like flint against steel. But I came to realize I was neither flint nor steel. After returning to West Marin, I was beginning to enjoy being flesh and blood and the curious enigma of being human.

And I came to realize that much of what I had experienced in my urban life were constructs about reality based upon how to exist in a highly demanding, competitive living environment. For instance, the art of Andy Warhol made perfect sense and was justifiably brilliant in its cool hipness, understanding of American commercialism, and historical place in art history. For me, however, in my innermost depths, the most amateurish but heartfelt painting of a sunset had more meaning and inspiration. My interest in the soulful thinking and feeling processes that went on inside people's minds far outweighed any enthusiasm I had for a commercial society or the art market.

By moving back to the Point Reyes Peninsula, I began to be filled with intense experiences that engaged my intellect, my senses, my entire being. Not being consumed by the ordeal of urban daily life meant that I could experience time in a different way. I still had to get things done by the rules of time that I experienced in New York, but it also meant I could experience time as ebb and flow, as cycles, and through my intuitive self. This suited my nature. I could be a silvery fish deep in a pool gently breathing in and out under the shelter of a rock, or a dolphin skipping across the rippling waves. I wasn't dependent upon how the outside world defined me as a professional artist. I had always felt that being an artist was a calling and not a career. Now I had the freedom to identify the ideas and beliefs that really mattered to me, and to pursue and explore the aspiration of my calling.

I found that by steeping myself in the location that had inspired me so much as a child, I was able to revisit my former sense of self, and instead of repressing it, add it to the bouquet of my life. Whether painfully thorny or ecstatically beautiful, I didn't feel the need to trim off any parts of it. By looking at the totality of the situation, all of the parts blended together in a richly integrated harmony. Like some of the garden roses that my mother had started from slips from California old-timers, the thorns were almost as large as the flowers. Danger and beauty created even greater splendor. Recently, I looked carefully at the vast array of new roses at a nursery and was disappointed to see that the thorns had been bred out of most of the roses. Like a tiger without claws, the element of ecstatic wildness, such an integral part of nature's beauty, had been tamed.

Being in this familiar landscape, I began to feel a sense of bedrock. I think humans are driven to find an innate sense of validity and significance. For me, this drive had sent me on a long journey to understand the meaning of humanity, spirit, integrity, and soul. Once, when I was 15, I remember sitting on a cliff near the Point Reyes Lighthouse. I was perched high above the ocean, ripped by winds and weather. I had burrowed beside the coyote brush and lupine, out of the wind, and looked out over the sea and rocks. As I gazed, the solidity of the rocks shifted into a different blueprint and I felt the infinite space between the molecules of what I was looking at. Slowly, everything shifted back to normal. Now I have the language to put sophistication to this moment, but then the feeling itself revealed that reality was made up of more space and lightness than I thought possible. My own journey has been developed from this ever-shifting paradigm of opposites. To feel substance, not rigid with control, but consisting of aliveness gathered together for a purpose, makes sense to me. Both were needed for me to develop my earthly presence.

In the urban environment in which I had lived for so long, the sounds and excess city stimulation meant I had to fight to be with my real creative concerns. Living in Point Reyes, I no longer experienced this pressure. I could walk outside and be in the very environment that nurtured my creativity. Now I no longer painted from mental constructs or ideas but from all of my emotions, senses, mind, and life experience.

Where the Sun Goes Down, 2006. Oil on linen. 11" × 16". Private collection.

In my urban life I was like a scientist trying to do astrophysics in a shopping mall; any experiments conducted in such an inappropriate setting would ensure flawed outcomes. Now I was in an unassuming, yet more forthright place. I finally felt I was in a laboratory that had all the right equipment for making good results.

When I moved back to Point Reyes in 1992, issues about the environment had not yet taken on the urgency of national interest they have now. The Marin Agricultural Land Trust (MALT) is an organization I feel close to because of its commitment to keeping agriculture and ranching in the West Marin. MALT is the first agricultural land trust in the United States, and it continues to be one of the most innovative organizations in keeping ranching and agricultural lands from being developed.

I support these endeavors because of my positive life experience of having grown up in a solid ranching community and my strong belief that ranchers, for the most part, have been excellent land stewards. I am convinced the ranching life style has much to offer in the way of modeling family cohesiveness, knowledge about food growing, conservation and animal husbandry.

Although the artistic world in West Marin is relatively small, it is vigorous and supportive. Many artists here share the beliefs that nature inspires, that man is a steward of the landscape, and that the interpretation of the landscape is a high calling. The beauty of this landscape can't help but affect anyone having interaction with it. The intensity of competition that sometimes occurs among artists is overridden here by support and mutual encouragement. For instance, a group of artists formed an annual open studios event, which is widely attended and during which many works of art are sold. By being truly oneself there is no competition anyway. After all, who could be you?

Chapter Eighteen

Within my limited means, I paint with as much courage as I can. Instead of reaching beyond my experience and limitations, I am thrilled to be able to paint the beauty of the world around me. Instead of reaching for an intellectual fabrication, I stretch deeply into the present moment. I praise and celebrate daily the sheer loveliness of the natural world, whether it is a slice of light falling between trees at the end of the day or the spectacular infinity of the ocean. Since my inner and outer environments now move in synchronization, there is a correlation, a response, a dialogue, and a meditation between my inner self and what I paint. The content is crucial to the meaning of the painting. It reveals my place in the artwork. This journey to the realization of beauty in form is my spiritual journey. My work has become simpler, yet takes longer to accomplish. It is more abstract, yet it is loaded with feeling. I want my paintings to reveal and strike a chord with the human condition, with its multiplicity, richness, and depth of feelings and vulnerability. This is the orchestra of human experience, from the most base to the most divine. This intense human experience invites me to appreciate and empathize with everything around me; this sensitivity helps me to protest when harmony and beauty are destroyed or degraded.

Cultivating an acute sense of being alive to the present moment is at the core of my creativity and I find that play and spontaneity nurture that energy. It seems to me that life is influenced and invigorated by intelligence and feeling but also has a presence of its own. To me, this is the heart of the Great Mystery. My job is to be able to step aside and let this happen. This is a transcendent process in the sense that what results is more than the sum of the parts. In other words, from the process a new reality occurs. It may have all of the traits and components it had before, but it becomes something new. The human mind may nurture this process to make it happen, but it cannot be created through human will or thinking alone.

My interest in painting landscapes began in 1980. I had a hunch then that landscape painting would take on a new vitality for me. I was teaching at the School of Skow-

hegan in Maine where I met several landscape painters from Baltimore. They were plein air painters who were painting directly from nature. I was impressed by their love of nature and the clarity of their vision. Their work had a sense of place and directness. They intrigued me since they were not intimidated by theories of modern art that absented the artist from the environment.

During that summer I thought a lot about the history of the United States and landscape painting. Early landscape painters like Bierdstadt presented an almost mythological grand view of the countryside. The primeval nature of America was endless and unknown. There was a common assumption that resources were endless and capable of magical replenishment. Western expansion constantly presented new landscapes for exploitation and habitation. The young painters I met in Skowhegan, however, were significant to me as *cherishers* of the landscape. I had a presentiment that they were the real new wave of artistic direction.

It seemed to me to be a natural arc from expansion, exploration, and exploitation of the resources of America, to cherishing and caring for the earth. Little did I know in the 1980s how prophetic this gut feeling was and how it would affect me. My trek back to the most western part of America gave me a new understanding of the need to cherish and steward what we already have. Cherishing, not exploiting, became my maxim.

I had a new understanding of the environment. By standing so clearly for what I believe in, I attract collectors who are drawn to my value system. I am now involved

Dana Hooper and me painting at Hamlet.   *Photos by Steve McKinney.*

Hamlet. 2000. Oil on canvas. 9" × 12". Collection of Peter and Elizabeth Evans.

with preserving the regionalism and diversity of the area and its environment. With another artist, Dana Hooper, also a native of Marin County, we put together several exhibitions about the tiny community of Hamlet on the eastern shore of Tomales Bay, hoping we could assist in the preservation of one of the oldest historic places in West Marin.

Judith Coburn, an investigative journalist, published a lengthy article about Hamlet and our endeavors in the *San Francisco Chronicle*. An old fishing settlement, some of its buildings had been hauled from great distances in the nineteenth century to perch on the waterside for habitation. Later in the early twentieth century it was a whistle stop on the narrow gauge railroad. At one time it had a hotel and post office. When I was growing up it had a thriving oyster business and a wonderful restaurant overlooking the bay. After the National Seashore began administering the property in the late 1980s, it slowly fell into ruins.

We were not successful in saving Hamlet, but we did awaken many people to the danger of destroying original rural architecture and housing structures in West Marin. Dana and I agree that the remnants of human history can be inspiration for the present and future. The past can be a model for the future. We loved these old simple unadorned structures, soulful in their hand-built usefulness. We strongly felt that

Rembrandt. *Aristotle Contemplating a Bust of Homer*. Image copyright © The Metropolitan Museum of Art/Art Resource, New York.

when these examples vanish, we are left inventing the new without the trial, error, and wisdom of time.

In taking responsibility for my life and utilizing new tools to express my true self, I'm learning to trust this process. This has been a transition to integration; the fulfillment of dreams and a time of new beginnings. The phase of my life since I returned to Point Reyes in 1992 is the most personal part of my story. Many of my struggles and contradictions have either become integrated or present themselves as challenges as opposed to threatening situations. I meditate in the morning and write ten things for which I am grateful. Then I write ten things I love and ten things in life that I praise. This is the core of my inner life. I feel that appreciation, love, and acknowledgement are ascending traits that nurture my spirit and the spirit of the world.

After a recent visit to New York, I thought about artwork that had affected me. What came to mind was the painting "Aristotle Contemplating a Bust of Homer" by Rembrandt in the Metropolitan Museum. I had visited the painting before but this time I was aware that my response was quite different. For the first time, I realized what moved me so deeply about this painting was that Rembrandt illuminated the breadth, depth, and substance of the human spirit, sincerely, humbly, and yet, divinely. Aside from the lofty title, I saw a man emerging from the darkness of his background, his face illuminated, yet his eyes strongly shadowed, perhaps through his life experience. His hand rests on the head of Homer, the two of them, one flesh and blood, and the other stone, in an unheard dialogue. The viewer can only speculate what this interchange is, but for me, I see that that the hand is resting compassionately and the entire composition is rooted in gravity and strength, which feels sacred in its aesthetic simplicity.

In the years since I returned to West Marin and for now, I feel I have a good balance between elements that I need in order to be creative and alive. Some of the topics of particular interest to me are: The relationship of beauty and self with the outer world; the expression of the divine in painting (and what is the divine?); and the manifestation and understanding of the Great Mystery. The following is from *Perfected Beings, Pure Realms*, an exhibition that was held at the Tibetan Museum in New York

City in 2006. The passage refers to Tibetan art, but it addresses the concept of beauty in a way that I feel encompasses many of my own thoughts.

> Without acknowledging a concept of beauty, apart from perfection of compassion, Himalayan art enlists the power of beauty to release us from our limited selves, if only for a moment. Truth, good and beauty are one. The grace afforded by a work of art is an opportunity for faith, and faith is a state of separation from ego that allows for a flowering of compassion. These works of art are soothing to the eye and reassuring to the troubled spirit. To the faithful, they are Buddha himself.

My life has been a quest. I was often searching for something for which there is no name, but it was coming from the deepest part of my cellular structure of being human. I may live to be 100, in which case this final chapter will have many more to follow. Or my life may be much shorter; in either case, I feel composure about where I am now. This serenity has to do with a certain knowingness about my human nature. Out of the unlimited bandwidth of life and consciousness, I am content with my limitations and weaknesses and celebrate the moving panorama of life.

Rising, Setting, 2009. Oil on linen. 24" × 36". Collection of Judith Ciani.

acknowledgments and gratitude

Judith Ayn Bernhard
Doug Cruikshank
Marie Dern
Chris Desser
Daidie Donnelly
Diana Divecha
Paul Gardner
Steve McKinney
Ian Toll
Yvonne Tsang
Deborah White

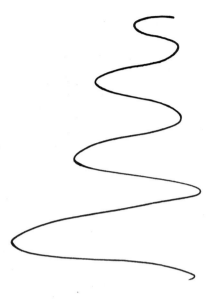

I keep following this sort of hidden river of my life,
you know, whatever the topic or impulse which comes,
I follow it along trustingly. And I don't have any sense
of its coming to a kind of crescendo, or of its
petering out either. It is just going steadily along.

— *William Stafford in a 1971 interview*